THE WORLD OF AUCTIONS

Where and How to Profit From Auctions

Douglas Caires & Richard Caires

The World of Auctions

AMERICAN AUCTION SERVICE, INC.

Copyright © 1993 by Richard Caires & Douglas Caires

All rights reserved under International and Pan American Copyright Conventions. Published in the U.S.A. by American Auction Service, Inc. No parts of this book may be used or reproduced in any matter whatsoever without written permission of American Auction Service, Inc, except in the case of brief quotations embodied in critical articles or reviews.

For any additional information, contact:

AMERICAN AUCTION SERVICE, INC.
Pier 40 West Houston Street
New York, New York 10014

ISBN 1-56171-281-7

Manufactured in the United States of America

10 9 8 7 6 5 4 3 2 1

Contents

FOREWORD 1

Part One

PART 1 CHAPTER 1 9
GUIDELINES FOR THE AUCTION BUYER

PART 1 CHAPTER 2 21
RESEARCHING THE AUCTION ASSET'S VALUE

PART 1 CHAPTER 3 37
THE AUCTION

PART 1 CHAPTER 4 43
TYPES OF AUCTIONS

PART 1 CHAPTER 5 49
METHODS OF BIDDING

PART 1 CHAPTER 6 55
BIDDING METHODS CHOSEN BY THE AUCTIONEER

PART 1 CHAPTER 7 59
OPEN TO THE PUBLIC

PART 1 CHAPTER 8 61
PAYING FOR YOUR PURCHASE

PART 1 CHAPTER 9 65
CONCLUDING YOUR PURCHASE

Part Two

PART 2 CHAPTER 1 79
THE UNITED STATES MARSHALS SERVICE

PART 2 CHAPTER 2 85
UNITED STATES CUSTOMS SERVICE

PART 2 CHAPTER 3 89
THE RESOLUTION TRUST CORPORATION

PART 2 CHAPTER 4 95
THE GENERAL SERVICES ADMINISTRATION (G.S.A.)

PART 2 CHAPTER 5 97
THE DEPARTMENT OF DEFENSE

PART 2 CHAPTER 6 99
THE INTERNAL REVENUE SERVICE

PART 2 CHAPTER 7 101
THE UNITED STATES POSTAL SERVICE

PART 2 CHAPTER 8 103
OTHER AGENCIES WHICH MAY AUCTION ASSETS

Part Three

PART 3 CHAPTER 1 109
UNITED STATES BANKRUPTCY COURT (USBC)

Part Four

PART 4 CHAPTER 1 117
REAL ESTATE TAX SALES

PART 4 CHAPTER 2 120
STATE AND LOCAL SURPLUS SALES

PART 4 CHAPTER 3 121
CITY MARSHAL SALES

PART 4 CHAPTER 4 123
SHERIFF SALES

PART 4 CHAPTER 5 125
POLICE SALES

PART 4 CHAPTER 6 127
SURPLUS CITY AND STATE OWNED REAL ESTATE

Part Five
STATE AND LOCAL JUDICIAL SOURCES OF AUCTIONS

INTRODUCTION 133

PART 5 CHAPTER 1 135
REAL ESTATE FORECLOSURE AUCTIONS

PART 5 CHAPTER 2 141
OTHER COMMON CAUSES FOR COURT ORDERED AUCTIONS

Part Six
PRIVATE SECTOR AUCTIONS

INTRODUCTION 147

PART 6 CHAPTER 1 149
WELL ESTABLISHED AUCTION HOUSES

PART 6 CHAPTER 2 151
PRIVATE SECTOR REAL ESTATE AUCTIONS

PART 6 CHAPTER 3 153
BANKS, FINANCE COMPANIES AND PRIVATE LENDERS

PART 6 CHAPTER 4 157
ALL OTHER SOURCES OF AUCTIONS

Part Seven
DIRECTORY OF FEDERAL AGENCIES

THE UNITED STATES MARSHALS 161

THE UNITED STATES CUSTOMS SERVICE 178

THE RESOLUTION TRUST CORPORATION 180

THE GENERAL
      SERVICES ADMINISTRATION (GSA) 186

THE DEPARTMENT OF DEFENSE 191

THE INTERNAL REVENUE SERVICE (IRS) 193

THE UNITED STATES POSTAL SERVICE 194

THE FEDERAL DEPOSIT
      INSURANCE CORPORATION 196

Part Eight
THE FEDERAL BANKRUPTCY COURT SYSTEM

THE FEDERAL BANKRUPTCY COURT 201
ADDRESSES OF UNITED STATES
    TRUSTEE FIELD OFFICES 202

FOREWORD

CONGRATULATIONS! You have taken the first step in discovering the world of auction liquidations. Whether you have never attended an auction or are a seasoned buyer, you will find the information presented in these pages to be extremely valuable. We have compiled a vast source of information for your convenience that will help you to find and attend auctions that are held for the assets that you may be interested in.

We at UNITED STATES AFFILIATES are in a unique position to be an authority on this subject. Our firm is a contracted auctioneer for the Federal Government. We have been handling Drug Seized Assets for the United States Department of Justice and the United States Marshal's Service for several years and are thoroughly familiar with all types of auctions. This experience has enabled us to compile this reference book to help potential auction participants find what they are looking for quickly and easily.

One of the comments I hear on a regular basis is: How do I find out about auctions? People ask me that question and hope I will give them the time honored secret of how to get in the inner circle of the auction world to get some bargain. Well, the secret is KNOWLEDGE! You do not have to be well connected with powerful business and political friends to attend an auction. You just have to know who holds them and when they are held. We will give you this knowledge.

You might have heard some people or other organizations promising you once in a lifetime opportunities at auctions. This is the exception rather than the rule. You will probably not be able to buy a Ferrari for $10 or a house for $15, but you should get excellent bargains at auctions. I personally

THE WORLD OF AUCTIONS

have made great deals at auctions. I paid $170,500 for my home in 1990, which is appraised at over $1,000,000 today. Notice that I didn't pay $15 for it. You also can expect to get a bargain at an auction, and that should be the premise that guides your bidding.

We have all heard the saying, "A penny saved is a penny earned." Well, I believe that saying doesn't hold true today. The fellow that coined that phrase so long ago didn't live in today's reality of federal, state and local income taxes. Let's talk about $100 saved. In order for you to be able to put $100 in the bank, how much would you have to earn? With the combination of federal, state and local taxes you may need to earn as much as $167 in gross pay in order take home and deposit a $100 into your bank. This is an EXTREMELY IMPORTANT POINT. We will show you how to buy assets at auction, save money on their purchase and, in effect, give yourself a raise on every purchase. Let me illustrate this point with the following examples. We will assume that you are about to purchase a used car from a dealer for a retail price of $10,000. Now if you were able to attend an auction that is selling a similar car and purchase the car for just the wholesale value of $9,000 you have made a significant deal. First, you are now the proud owner of the car you wanted. Second, you have been able to save $1,000 of the money you were willing to spend on the car at the dealer's. That $1,000 that is still in your bank is as if you gave yourself a raise of $1,670 dollars because that is the amount you would need to earn in order to have $1,000 in the bank. Every dollar that you save on the purchase of an asset is a significant boost to your net worth. If the asset that you are buying is a house, a savings of $10,000 would be like getting a $16,700 raise, and you still get to own the asset you want to buy. These examples are conservative. You will see assets sold at some auctions at far below market values, thereby increasing your savings. It is not uncommon to see cars sell for 50% of retail prices every day. Where do you think those car dealers get their cars from?

If you are a business owner the impact of this argument is multiplied! In order for you to put $100 in your personal account you must get paid $167, before taxes, from your company. What amount of goods and services must your company sell to generate $167 net? If your company operates on a 20% profit margin then it would have to record sales of $835 in order to pay you $167. This example does not take into account business taxes.

This clearly illustrates the fact that businesses should take every opportunity to save money on the acquisition of business assets. The money saved stays right on your bottom line. The opportunities to acquire everything from basic office supplies to entire companies or divisions are out there waiting for the sharp businessman to take advantage of them.

I know of a man in the excavating business. We had spoke on occasion and he told me he needed to acquire a new bulldozer. I told him there are many auctions for construction equipment and that I would keep an eye open for him. I found an auction that might have the type of machinery that he was looking for and informed him. He attended this auction and was able to buy the same model machine that he was willing to pay $105,000 for from some dealer, for only $65,000. This man got the asset he wanted and saved $40,000 on its purchase. He would have to work long and hard to make that $40,000 he saved.

This book will give you the knowledge that you need to get involved in the auction world to the extent you desire. I know many people that have established a very lucrative business in the buying and resale of assets from auctions. You may also find this to be a viable method to increase your income.

I know of a case where a man wanted to buy a house and move his family out of the small rental apartment which they were living in. He had bad credit, a limited income and no savings to be used as a down payment. I told him that the first thing he must do is get the $10,000 down payment he needed for the house. He would have had a long hard time to save that amount of money from his $35,000 per year job. Since he had limited funds and was mechanically inclined he began to purchase and resell some cars that he had bought at auction. He followed our advice of the asset value research and set his bid prices accordingly. He would buy cars that would sell for below wholesale and then resell them for close to retail levels. It doesn't take long to accumulate $10,000 when you earn a $800 to $1,500 profit on each transaction. In a matter of weeks he was able to accumulate the $10,000 he needed. But it gets better; he was able to find a house in the neighborhood he wanted that was sold at auction at a price equal to 70% of the general prices on that block. You can also do this in your spare time and improve your situation.

Some people say to me that they are afraid to take the risk of buying an item like a car for resale. I suggest to people of this nature to look at the purchase of the auctioned car as if they were buying themselves a newer used car. If they research the price and stick to their predetermined bid, then they will own a car at a good price and use it while the try to resell it for the profit that was built into their predetermined bid price. In any event it should play out to a no lose situation.

The potential for profit is unlimited in this field. One man bought some property at a NYC surplus real estate auction for $35,000 and sold it unimproved one year later for $350,000. The City of New York even gave the man a 7% mortgage for the original purchase when prevailing rates were over

10%. Another man, who is in the carpet business bought a huge inventory of carpet at a bankruptcy auction for a fraction of its cost. A carpet that would retail for $34 per yard was purchased through auction for $4 per yard. He bought thousands of yards. He told me that he would make more money on the carpets he bought that day then he made over the last three years.

We constantly hear people tell us of the deals they got on various items. One of the more interesting auctions we held was for the assets that came from the military PX in the Philippines that was destroyed by the Mt. Pinatubo volcano. The salvage firm that bought the assets from the insurance company brought about a $4,000,000 inventory to New Jersey for liquidation. The majority of the assets were sold at wholesale prices to the public, but about $300,000 of assets remained and had to be sold so that they could vacate the building they were storing the assets in. As it turned out, on the day of the auction there was a snow storm which kept the crowd to a handful. Those people got great deals. One woman bought six shopping carts filled to the top with high quality pens for $100 per cart. I estimated that each cart had 2,000 pens in it, which turned out to be 5 cents per pen. Everything at this auction went cheap. The examples of everyday people who have made significant money through auctions would fill this book. We will give you the knowledge you need to understand the auction world and help you get started on the path to saving your hard earned money on the purchase of assets or to serve as an income producing occupation for you.

I cannot stress enough the importance of researching the value of the items being sold. One man who attended one of our auctions for drug-seized property bought two banged up dragster racing motorcycles for $1,000 apiece. I asked him what he was going to do with them and he told me he bought them just for the engines, which he said were worth about $20,000 apiece. This man did his homework and realized the true value of these bikes when everybody else didn't have a clue.

You will find some helpful hints in this book to assist you in determining the value of the assets you are interested in. You must keep your head at an auction and keep to predetermined price guidelines you have set for yourself to insure you do not overpay for an item. Sometimes assets are sold for more than they are worth, but the buyer may place an emotional added value on the item. This is acceptable as long as you are not planning to resell for a profit. In general try to get a deal. You will feel better about it.

Finally, I suggest that you use the knowledge that we have carefully assembled for you to your benefit. Whether you are looking to purchase a car, boat, plane, house, fine art, collectibles, business asset or general merchandise, attending an auction for those items is not only interesting and potentially lucrative, but it is also fun. Sooner or later almost anything you can imagine will come up for auction, so you are bound to find something that interests you. We believe this book will be of great help to you and sincerely wish you GOOD LUCK.

Part One

PART 1

CHAPTER 1

GUIDELINES FOR THE AUCTION BUYER

The first decision you must make is what type of asset you would like to own. I advise people to examine the purchases they are planing to make in the near future as a starting point. If you need a car, boat or a home, take some time to clarify your requirements for these assets and WRITE THEM DOWN. This simple task of clarifying your thoughts, needs and desires and putting them down on paper will help you enormously in your search to fulfil your GOALS.

We will assume that you have decided that you would like to buy a house. You should clarify this desire as to the neighborhood, size, design, number of rooms, number of baths and condition of the house you would find acceptable. You should also determine if this is to be used as a residence, a rentable or a turnover investment, either long or short term. You will most probably find your requirements for a rental or an investment property to be a bit more relaxed than for a house to be used as your residence.

You should also consider the financial aspects of your contemplated purchase. This will help you fine tune your requirements and help you in searching for this asset. Consult with your accountant as to your ability to carry the costs of a house. You should consider the following as a bare minimum:

THE WORLD OF AUCTIONS

a) Down payment ability.

b) Maximum purchase price that you can carry.

c) Mortgage availability (see chapter 8).

d) Real estate taxes: these can vary widely from town to town.

e) Potential rental income.

f) Resale potential.

g) Consult your ATTORNEY.

Once you have carefully considered all of these items a clear picture of the asset you desire will develop. Now you must find an auction which has assets that fit your parameters. I must insist that you attend auctions for assets that you may initially assume are beyond your reach financially. You may be pleasantly surprised to find that you wind up owning a house that you had thought unattainable. You should always be ready and able to take advantage of an opportunity that may come your way. You never know what may happen in an auction, so reach for the stars, you may catch one for the price you want to pay.

It is vitally important to become aware of auctions. The saying "You've got to be in it to win it" is the truth. You must know when and where the auctions will be held. You can look in the Table of Contents for the various agencies holding auctions and how to contact them. Consult the chapters in this book that deal with the assets you are interested in and follow the guidelines on contacting the proper party that would handle the auction. Also note the methods of advertisement that are employed and get in the habit of looking through them. For example, in New York, the New York Times Sunday edition has the last pages of section 11 reserved for auction advertising. You should call all of your local papers and ask them when and where they publish auction advertisements. In addition, look through published legal notices on a daily basis. Many government agencies publish notices of the forfeiture of assets in the Wednesday edition of U.S.A. TODAY. These notices will not give you any auction information but they will tell you what agency and district is handling a particular asset. Use this information, including a full description and case number, to contact the agency in the manner described in this book in later chapters.

Once you have contacted the potential auction sources and have gotten into the routine of reviewing their auction advertisements, you are ready to do your research on the assets being auctioned. Your research will examine the assets' value, inspection of conditions and the review of title transfer method.

The methods of research are detailed in latter chapters, but this research will lead to the establishment of a BID PRICE LIMIT.

Whenever you go to an auction you should set predetermined bid price limits for the assets you want. This price will represent a percentage of the value of the asset. This percentage will vary for every person because it reflects the personal opinion of the individual buyer. Some people will use published wholesale/retail guides to help them establish a price limit for an asset. Other people use comparable sales, such as in real estate, to establish a limit. Still other people decide not to establish a limit and are determined to own an asset. They use the auction bidding process to establish an "instant market" for the assets value; this is common in the worlds of Art, Antiques and Collectables.

Your price limit should reflect your intent for the asset. If you are looking at an asset with the idea of a short term investment or a quick resale in mind, then you had better set your price limit at a point where you have some equity built into you purchase price. For instance, if you are looking at a car that has a retail price of $10,000 and a wholesale price of $8,500, you should determine how much profit you want to make if you are able to resell the car for retail. Some people would tend to say that they would pay wholesale for the car, but I want you to know that "wholesale" is just a guideline. You can go to many auctions and never see prices even approach wholesale. So, set a price limit that you feel comfortable with and DO NOT GO OVER IT!

The policy of setting a bidding limit for yourself will help you avoid that dreaded disease called AUCTION FEVER. I can't tell you how many times I have seen people lose their minds at an auction. Sometimes the disease manifests itself as an uncontrollable urge to throw ones money away. Other symptoms make certain people determined to outbid the competition without regard to the value of the asset that is being bid on. These people that suffer from AUCTION FEVER and buy assets as a result normally experience another disease called BUYERS REMORSE the following day which may last for weeks.

With all kidding aside, you must keep your head at an auction. If you follow my advice, and you should, you will have established a bid price limit based on a careful examination of many criteria. Do you think you should ignore this limit for a price that may be determined in a split second at an auction? I have seen some people pay more for used cars than a new one would have cost. The only explanation for such a thing is that they had no idea of the asset's value or they got caught up in a bidding war or they thought that their was a million dollars of some drug dealer's money hidden under the seat or they were just plain ignorant. I do not want this to happen to anyone who reads this book. KEEP YOUR HEAD AT AN AUCTION!

An auctioneer is a salesman whose job is to get you to pay as much as he can get for the asset. Since most auctioneers are paid on a commission basis, their earnings are totally dependant on what you pay. Some auctioneers employ BID ASSISTANTS, whose job it is to get you to keep bidding. Not only will you be tempted by the atmosphere of the auction to raise your price, but you may have one of these guys whispering in your ear with advice like: "Don't lose it!" or "Come on, don't quit now!" or "Keep going, your a good bidder". The last compliment you want to hear is that you are a good bidder from an auctioneer. All of these methods that are employed at auctions have been developed over generations for the sole purpose of getting your price up. That is why it is vitally important to follow my advice on setting and sticking to predetermined bid price limits. Chapters 3 and 5 will give more information on this subject.

The physical inspection of an asset that is going to be auctioned is very important and potentially difficult. In order to accurately estimate the value of any asset you must do your best to determine the condition of that asset. Most auctions specify an inspection time to view the assets. Unfortunately, quite often all you can do is view them. Cars are routinely sold without being started and with only a two hour inspection period allowed for 100 cars. Boats are often sold while they are sitting on dry dock and planes are sold while parked on a runway with only the maintenance logs to review if you are lucky. Real estate is sold with only one or two viewing dates provided, which may not be enough time to get an engineer or termite inspector in. So what do you do? The answer is reflected in your bid price. You must bid with the knowledge that you were only able to kick the tires and not take it around the block. This is one of the main reasons why you can buy assets at low prices at auctions. Take this into account when you are setting your bid price limit. You must anticipate potential problems and hope you don't find any.

In my experience as an auctioneer I have seen thousands of assets sold and have heard of very few problems. You can get a pretty good idea as to what you are buying within the time frame allotted. If you are not able to determine the condition of an asset by yourself, I suggest that you bring someone with you who may be able to help you.

When you hear in the Terms and Conditions of a sale; AS IS, WHERE IS, you must be aware that you are about to buy something that is in its present condition. Whatever that condition is, you own it and have to live with it without recourse. This fact should also be considered when setting your bid price limits. The unknown condition element is something you must deal

Where and How To Profit From Auctions

with to a certain extent whenever you buy something without the benefit of a guarantee. There is an element of risk involved with every purchase, but the risk should be justified by the reward if you set your prices correctly.

Many items are sold without an inspection time for all practical purposes. The military sells surplus items which are stored in various facilities around the country. You can bid on these assets through the mail from across the country without even seeing them. The only thing you have to go by, in most cases, is a one or two sentence description of the asset and a representation of its condition. It may read as follows: 1,200 dozen; men's shirts; color white; condition new. This information is what you are to base your bid on, so you must price them accordingly.

Try to get as much information as you can about an asset. It will help you make an informed decision and give you an edge over someone who did not do the proper research. Knowledge is the key to the auction business, so get as much as you can and reading this book is a giant step in the right direction. We will provide you with knowledge that will give you an edge over someone who didn't read this book. We will show you the tricks of the trade.

Many people who ask me about auctions are surprised to hear my next recommendation. My advice to them in regard to their first auction is to go through the auction as a "DRY RUN". They should follow all my techniques and suggestions but DO NOT BUY at your first auction. I suggest that you leave your home with a single dollar in your pocket. I say this to help you avoid being added to the list of people who have bought things at their first auction that they didn't want, need or wish they had bought. I want you to get familiar with how an auction feels so that you will have a good experience. You will find that auction going will be a fun experience for you when you are aware of what is going on around you. As with any business, when you are a newcomer you are bound to find out things the hard way. I will help you avoid some of the potential problems.

One of the most important portions of an auction is the beginning, when the TERMS AND CONDITIONS are read. This portion of the sale will outline the requirements and responsibilities of the buyer, the auctioneer and the agency or principal that the auctioneer is acting for. You must pay special attention to this segment since terms and conditions and other announcements from the podium take precedence over previous terms and conditions, even written ones. The terms and conditions will constitute a contract between the buyer and the auctioneer, either written or verbal. For the most part, terms and condition address acceptable payment methods and time restrictions of such payment. Make sure you understand all terms and conditions before you make a deposit or pay for an item. You may have a problem if you do not have the proper form of payment tendered in the proper time. You could even lose your deposit. If the terms require you to close in thirty days you better be able to do that. Also, you may find real estate sales not to be subject to you obtaining a mortgage. Real estate sales can be very complex and you should retain the services of an attorney.

In regard to the titles that are to be transferred for vehicles, you should pay special attention. Some auctions, like the ones we handle for the Federal government, will guarantee free and clear title and issue you a Federal title which is accepted by state motor vehicle offices without question. Some auctions will sell you only the Rights, Title and Interest in a vehicle or asset. With this type of sale you assume any and all liens on the asset. Most state and city governments sell the vehicles they seize for traffic and parking related offenses in this manner. The I.R.S. sells most of the property it seizes in this manner. This may turn out to be a problem for you if you do not do your homework. You must research the liens and establish the amount of equity left in the asset. Some municipalities and even the Federal government will, on occasion, research the liens and guarantee that they found all of them. In that case you can feel comfortable with purchasing such assets. The only thing you should still be concerned with in this case is title transfer. The laws differ from state to state, so get a clear understanding of how long it will take you to get title in your name. If title transfer is a matter of days, that should not influence your bid price. However, if title transfer takes several weeks, then you should figure that in and lower your bid price. Any contingency that will delay your ability to own, register or resell the asset should be considered negatively when determining your bid.

As a general rule of thumb, you should be able to get the terms and conditions for big ticket items that require the assistance of professionals, like lawyers and accountants, well in advance of the sale. The selling agency will do the leg work, in most cases, to take the risk out of the purchase of the assets they are trying to sell. They will do this to insure they get the highest dollar price for the assets they are selling. I suggest that you call either the auctioneer or the principal the auctioneer is working for to get the terms and conditions in advance.

In some instances where the asset is substantial and its disposition is being handled by a court appointed referee or by a judge directly, as is the case in Bankruptcy cases, the potential bidder may have some leverage in shaping the terms and conditions of the sale. This is especially true when the court is trying to sell a company as a whole in an effort to save the jobs of the employees which would certainly be lost if the company were to be dismantled and auctioned off in pieces. The bidder may find himself in a position to demand terms beyond the court's control. Some examples would include debt restructuring with creditor banks, stock restructuring with share holders and wage and benefit concessions from the labor force. The motivation of all the players mentioned above is strong since they probably have more to gain with the entity's restructuring than its demise.

There are a few things I would like to point out for you to be aware of. Many auctions contain the term and condition "buyer's premium". This is a method of payment for the auctioneer which adds on his commission to the sale price. If you see a 10% buyers premium and you bid $100 for an item, you will be required to pay an additional $10 to the auctioneer for a total of $110. This may seem rather straightforward and simple, but the truth of the matter is that the majority of people forget to figure the buyers premium into their bid prices.

The fact that most people forget about the buyer's premium is why it is so popular to auctioneers and the principals they represent. Suppose you were a company that wanted to sell off some surplus goods at auction. Let's assume you hoped they would sell for $100,000. Now you must hire an auctioneer who wants a 10% commission. If the company agrees, then it would net $90,000 on the auction. If the company is hesitant about the commission structure the auctioneer then offers the following deal to the company. The auctioneer will not get paid from the proceeds but from the buyers with a 10% buyer's premium. In the school I went to you would assume that the company would get the same result; that the assets that should sell for $100,000 would now be bid up to only slightly more than $90,000 because everyone would remember to figure in the auctioneer. Well guess what? Lets say half of the people remember to figure in the 10%, so they adjust their bids to total $45,000 and the other half forgets to figure in the buyer's premium and their bids total $50,000. So in this case the company gets a net amount of $95,000 and is happy, and the auctioneer gets paid $9,500 from the buyers and he's happy also.

The above example is why buyers premiums are around. It is a method of marketing auction services that is more palatable to a firm that is cost conscious and at the same time keeps the proceeds paid to the auctioneer as high as possible. This method only works at the expense of auction buyers who are not aware of what is going on. Now that you have read this and are aware of this practice make sure that you always figure in the buyer's premium when you are setting your bid price limits. My readers should always save those extra percentage points after reading this. I sometimes wonder how much money this advice adds up to. Remember, a buyer's premium will take advantage of the uninformed, not my readers.

The subject of CON JOBS is an area which always disturbs me. As with any business there exists a segment who believes that ripping you off is easier than being upstanding and honest. The vast majority of auction houses and auction sales make every effort to insure that the auction buyer is treated fairly. Established auction houses depend on return business from auction buyers which they would not receive if they were not honest.

However, there are con jobs out there that I will give you some pointers on how to identify them and avoid them. All sales where the principal or auction sponsor is a state, local government, federal agency or court ordered are all above board. When you get into the private sector is when you must be careful.

Every week I see adds for "Emergency Cargo Liquidation" of Persian and Oriental Rugs which must be sold off immediately at auction to head off some impending financial disaster. Or they state that the disaster has already taken place and they are overstocked or even GOING OUT OF BUSINESS. I often wonder why someone would even get into a business that is always a disaster in the first place. These entities somehow manage to be in trouble every week. Don't believe it. They try to appeal to your greed and make you think you can get a great deal from a desperate seller. They, in fact, are not desperate but prosperous and their adds should read: "going out FOR business ".

Another common ploy is what I call the "copy cat auction", where an auction is set up to look, taste and smell like a real auction from U.S. Customs or some other bona fide auction sponsor. These are, in fact, cons to get you to come to an auction to buy their goods which have nothing to do with any drug seizure, legal action or court order at all. Used car wholesalers sometimes set these up to move their merchandise. It is easy to identify these, just ask them directly what type of title you receive. Any vehicle we sell for the United States Department of Justice will get a title from the UNITED STATES GOVERNMENT because the seized and forfeited cars are owned by the government. If the title they offer is anything but this then you know that you are not dealing with the federal government. You should GO HOME! If you wind up in one of these auctions you can get an idea that something isn't exactly right during the bidding. You may see the bidding escalate rather quickly when it seems that no one is really bidding. You may find yourself bidding against a SHILL who is an individual in the crowd who is connected with the auctioneer and his function is to raise the bids. I have even seen some of these so called auctioneers use an imaginary bidder. They ask for a price and point to an empty car and say they got it. If you find yourself in one of these situations, GO HOME! Another thing to be aware of is an auction that advertises excessively. Most real auctions only have a small budget set aside to advertise. In fact, they only advertise to the extent that they are required to by law, which is a legal notice in two local publications. If you start seeing big print ads, or worse yet hearing radio ads, then STAY HOME! To summarize, look for the following:

- a) Try to go to auctions that are sponsored by real governments or their agencies.

- b) Try to go to auctions that are held at established auction houses.

- c) Beware of look alike or copy cat auctions.

- d) Beware of advertisements to avoid some disaster.

- e) Beware of any auction that advertises excessively.

- f) Beware of auctions where the bidding seems rigged.

- g) Check with the Better Business Bureau and your local Department of Consumer Affairs or your state's Attorney General to see if these places have complaints on file. Do not use the lack of complaints as an endorsement, since these operations commonly take on new corporate identities.

- h) Use your common sense!

You can avoid these types of auctions by using your common sense. This is an area of concern to all honest auctioneers, and I want my readers to be educated and aware of this problem. These rotten apples are a very small portion of the industry that you must avoid. If you happen to encounter one of them I suggest that you contact your local Department of Consumer Affairs or the Better Business Bureau or your state Attorney Generals office and file a complaint.

Whenever you attend an auction, I suggest you take a few minutes to inquire about a mailing list that may be maintained by the auctioneer. Most auctioneers charge a nominal amount for their mailing list. Since it is important to know when and where an auction will be held, the more information you have the more educated you become. It will be less likely for an auction to slip by you with assets in it that you would want to bid on if you increase the amount of auction information you receive. It is also a good idea to ask the auctioneer or his staff where and when they advertise the auctions that they handle. In later chapters of this book you will find descriptions of various sponsors of auctions and how to contact them. Please follow these instructions. They are designed to save you leg work and frustration.

I endorse the use of professionals to assist you in your dealings with auctions. Most auctions you can probably handle yourself. When you get into big ticket items such as real estate, art and businesses there are times when it would be prudent to employ a professional to assist you with legal and accounting matters.

If you are contemplating the purchase of real estate that will require an all cash immediate closing or a 30 day closing, I suggest that you contact your attorney before the auction to alert him of his impending service. You must be prepared to meet all the terms and conditions set at an auction to successfully conclude your purchase. One of the terms that could cause you a problem is the time limits set to conclude your transaction. Make sure that you get everything lined up to meet the terms and pay special attention to the time constraints.

The time constraints put on sales of real estate and other assets may seem to make the auction more difficult for the buyer. This is true, because you must act quickly in an area where transactions would normally be concluded in a much longer time period. The average non-auction real estate sale closes between 60 to 90 days after a contract is signed. With an auction of real estate it is common practice to close the sale in 30 days from the auction date. This is one of main contributing factors as to why you can get a bargain on real estate at an auction. In addition, the fact that only a limited number of people know about a piece of property being auctioned as compared to the number of people that would be aware of a piece of property being handled by a broker in multiple listings also contributes to lower competition for auctioned property. These circumstances will work out to your benefit if your prepare for them.

Payment terms are an area where people make mistakes that can cost them the opportunity to bid. This can be easily avoided. All auctions specify in advance in their advertisements the payment or deposit requirements. If they want deposits in bank checks only, bring them a bank check, not a personal check, money order or food stamps. Make sure you make the check payable as specified by the auctioneer. If they want it made out to Acme Auctions or to a government agency, follow their guidelines. Do not make a check payable to yourself and try to endorse it over to the auctioneer. They probably would not accept this unless they specified this to be acceptable. Do not make a check payable to an individual unless you have the merchandise you bought in your possession. If they want cash bring cash and not something "as good as cash". Failure to follow their instruction will probably eliminate you from bidding. It always seems to work out that on the occasion you are excluded from bidding because of something so simple as making a check out improperly is the day when the assets being auctioned off go for next to nothing. So please pay attention to these little details.

People ask me this question at every auction: "How do I know how much of a deposit to bring?" We require a 20% deposit on all purchases. I tell them to bring enough money to insure that they will be able to meet the deposit requirements of the maximum price they are willing to spend. For example: if you only want to spend $10,000 for an item, bring at least $2,000 with you. My readers will recognize this as identifying your bid price limit and bringing the appropriate amount of funds with you. Then I get the question: "What happens if I bring more than the $2,000 I need?" (I really do get these questions.) It doesn't matter, in this case, if you overpay your deposit because you still have to pay the balance in a few days anyway. The only concern you should have is if you do not bring enough to meet the deposit requirements or if the item sells for less than the amount of your deposit check. In that case the auctioneer will refund the difference to you or hold your check until you issue him another one for the proper amount. To avoid this slight potential of a problem you should just bring several smaller checks with you.

Another procedural area that may cost you the opportunity to participate and bid in an auction is registration. At some auctions you are required to register with the auctioneer to be entitled to bid. The registration requirement will vary from auction to auction. You may be required to give the name, address and phone number, or the requirements can be expanded and actually become restrictive. The act of registration also reinforces the contract between the auctioneer and the buyer. The terms and conditions are often written on the back of the registration form and your signing the form will state that you will abide by them.

It is not uncommon for registration and admittance to be contingent on the prospective bidder to show proof of a required deposit that must be paid if you are the winning bidder. Real estate auctions commonly require bidders to bring a check with them for as little as a $1,000 to as much as $50,000 or more to register to bid. No check - No admission! This could be a problem for you if you did not pay attention to the terms and conditions in the auction advertisements. It is a simple matter to avoid this by carefully reading the advertisement a few times. If you are unsure, contact the auctioneer and get a clarification of their requirements.

PART 1

CHAPTER 2

RESEARCHING THE AUCTION ASSET'S VALUE

Researching the value of an asset that is going to be sold at an auction is probably the most important thing that you must do when you go to an auction. Most of the auctions you will be exposed to will only be selling one or two types of assets, such as cars and boats, or art work and business assets. You will find auctions, such as estate auctions, that will sell off the entire contents of a home that can have just about anything in it. But most auctions deal with an asset type that a government agency may have control over, like drug seized vehicles. Or perhaps the auction will deal with a business bankruptcy case where all of the firm's furniture, fixtures and inventory will be sold off.

This fact will work in your favor when you start to research asset values. You will only need to focus on one subject matter at a time, and thereby be less inclined to make a mistake. If you are attending an auction for cars, boats, coins or whatever, we will give you some advice on setting your bid price limit. Some assets are easier to research than others. You will find all kinds of publications to help you with vehicles, boats, planes and coins, but other assets like real estate, art, business concerns and business assets are more difficult because there is no accepted pricing guides for them. Their value must be determined on an individual basis using a variety of methods including the employment of professionals.

I have seen too many cases were people look into the value of an asset and make only one mistake in doing so. It's a big mistake! They find out the value of an asset AFTER they bought it. They may be lucky and discover they made a good purchase or they may find that they bought a real dog for an inflated price. Whatever the outcome is, their method of purchase was flawed. Please make an effort to determine values before the sale, during the inspection period. I always see people leafing through pricing guides while the actual bidding is taking place. If you do this you will not be able to concentrate on the bidding and all the activity around you. So do your homework before you start bidding. We will give you some guidelines below to help you determine values.

VEHICLES

If you want to by a used car at an auction you should make a small investment in a used car price guide. There are quite a few publications for you to choose from. Depending on your intent, you should choose a publication that will suit your needs. If you are just going to the auction to buy a second car for your kid then a store bought guide will do. It will give you the basic values you will require such as the wholesale and retail prices. Make sure that the guide you choose will cover the model year you are interested in. Most of these guides only span a 10 year period, so double check to see if you are buying the correct guide. If you are going to get serious about buying and selling cars I would suggest one of the more thorough guides. These are published more frequently and give you more detailed information, such as V.I.N. numbers and trim package numbers, etc. They are sold on a subscription basis and are required reading for any serious buyer.

The value of any asset, especially a car, is largely dependent on its condition. The prices quoted in the price guide books reflect the value of a car in excellent condition and mileage for its age. You must deduct money for things like high mileage, poor mechanical condition, body damage and worn tires. When it comes to a used car you have to have an "eye" for problems. The ability to detect the history of a car just by looking at it comes from experience and not from any summary advice I could give you. You can get a basic idea of what to look for by reading some pointers that were given to me by a professional auction car buyer who buys about 10 cars from me at each of our United States Marshal sales.

I must tell you a story about this man. I own a rare car, a Jensen Interceptor that I had brought to one of my auctions. This car was in original condition except for a repair to the fender of a small dent that a parking attendant gave me. I had it fixed at an excellent body shop and I could not tell that it was ever damaged. Everybody I know could not tell that it was damaged. Well, he saw my car from about twenty feet away and said to me after about two seconds: "Gee, it got hit on that fender." I couldn't believe he was able to detect that, but his experience enabled him to see problems that mere mortals wouldn't have a clue about. He gave me some advice to be incorporated in this book.

1) If you can arrange for a professional car buyer or a mechanic to come to the auction with you, do it.

2) Stand back from the car and look at the paint. Observe any color differences form one body panel to another. If you detect a difference it means the car had a problem and it was repaired. The problem might have been a big one like hitting a wall or something as small as fixing some scratches.

3) Do the magnet trick. Bring a magnet, preferably one from the front of your refrigerator because these are not too strong. Run the magnet around the car. If it sticks, then you have metal. If it falls off then you have found body work and a potential problem.

4) Bring a flashlight! You can't find problems if you can't see them.

5) Look for rust. Look under the wheel wells, under the door frames and under the rugs to get a look at the floor boards. If you see rust you should feel a tug on your wallet because it will be just a matter of time before it will get unsightly and require a repair.

6) It may be difficult to determine the condition of the engine and drive train of a vehicle being sold at an auction because many times they are not started. In these circumstances look at the appearance of the engine. If it is spotless and all the hoses are shiny then you are looking at an engine that has been cleaned up and you should be suspicious. Check the oil, look at the dip stick. If the oil is new be suspicious; if it is grey then walk away because that means that there is water mixing with the oil. Smell it, note any burnt odor. Rub the oil between your fingers and feel for grit. If you find any negative results you may be looking at some type of engine trouble or neglect or an attempt to cover it up.

7) If the cars are not started look inside the tail pipe. If it is rusty then the car has not been running for some time. This in itself may not be unusual since many cars that are seized will be stored while the court cases proceed. It is not uncommon for a

car to be stored for a year or longer while legal matters are pending. If you rub your finger inside the pipe and find an oily residue then you are looking at a car that burns oil. Gray or black soot is preferred.

8) If the cars will be started then you should first determine that the engine is cold before they start. Sometimes the cars are warmed up before inspection to make them run better when they are started for the bidders. When the car is started listen carefully to determine how easily it starts and how it runs. Look at the exhaust for signs of blue smoke: that means trouble.

9) Look at the tires. If they have uneven wear then you will need front end repairs. Note a car that has low mileage and bald tires: you may be looking at a lemon trying to look like an apple.

10) Look under the car for signs of leaks of oil and water.

These basics will help determine the condition of a vehicle. If you can get a professional to come with you, that would be advisable. You should set your prices based upon your inspection and the price guide books. DO NOT BID ON A CAR YOU HAVE NOT INSPECTED! Below I will list some publications of pricing guides for both the one time buyer and the full time buyer. These books are available in a subscription form or at a book store.

PRICE GUIDE BOOKS FOR THE ONE TIME BUYER

If you are looking to buy a car for your personal use I would suggest purchasing a store-bought priving guide. They are available at book stores and at full service auto part stores. These books cost less than $5.00 and are definitely worth the money.

They are normally updated every two to three months to reflect price changes. One good one is EDMUNDS USED CAR PRICES, and it will give you wholesale and retail prices for foreign and domestic cars and light trucks for the past ten years. Another publisher that deserves mention is PACE PUBLICATIONS. They issue several pricing guides, one of which should focus on the car you are interested in.

PRICE GUIDE BOOKS FOR THE SERIOUS BUYER

A professional buyer, someone that will buy and sell for profit, needs all the information he can get to make good decision when buying a vehicle. For these buyers I would strongly suggest subscribing to one or more of the following pricing guides.

One published book is the National Automobile Dealer Association (NADA) Official Used Car Guide. They publish this monthly and by region. This is an excellent guide with detailed information on all the cars in it. You can contact NADA as follows:

NATIONAL AUTOMOBILE DEALERS
USED CAR GUIDE COMPANY
8400 Westpark Drive
McLean, VA 22102-9985
Cost of Subscription: $43 annually
Telephone number: 703-821-7193
Toll free number inside Virginia: 800-523-3110
Toll free number outside Virginia: 800-544-6232

NADA publishes several other guides that you may wish to subscribe to. One of them will summarize prices based on auto auction sale results. It is titled: Official Used Car Trade-In Guide. This guide is updated every two weeks and will get even more detailed. It will break down the prices for cars by their condition.

Cost of subscription: $44 annually.

NADA also publishes:

1) A guide for older cars which is updated every four months and costs $45 annually.

2) Official Mobile Home Guide which is updated every four months and costs $90 annually.

3) A guide for motorcycles, snowmobiles and jet skis, etc. which is updated every four months and costs $45 annually.

4) A recreational vehicle guide which is updated every four months and costs $90 annually.

Another publisher of professional pricing guides is:

MacLean Hunter Market Reports, Inc.
P.O. Box 6500
Chicago, IL 60608
Telephone: 312-726-2802
Toll Free: 800-621-9907

This company publishes the "RED" & "BLUE" books. Contact them for the appropriate publication for the vehicles you are interested in. Their prices range from $47 and up for annual subscriptions.

Another publisher of pricing guides for the professional that is gaining recognition is:

Galves Auto Price List, Inc.
430 Industrial Ave.
Teterboro, N.J. 07608
Telephone: 201-393-0051
Fax: 201-393-0508

Galves' publishes several pricing guides but I would recommend their Basic American & Foreign. This updates the American cars weekly and the foreign cars monthly. The cost of subscription is $80.

EXOTIC CARS

If you are interested in making an investment in an exotic car I would suggest that you buy the C.P.I. Guide which stands for Cars Of Particular Interest. This guide will help you determine the value of your dream car. You can reach them as follows: 301-317-4228

The CPI guide will cost only twenty dollars annually and it is updated quarterly.

These books are essential if you are going to buy a car at an auction. Even if you at not attending an auction and go to a used car dealer, the specter of a customer in the showroom with one of these publications will send shivers down the spine of the salesman. These guides will help to keep you from being taken. Get in the habit of researching the values of all assets you are interested in and set a bid price limit for yourself based on the numbers in the guides and the condition of the vehicle.

I wish to inform my readers that the prices you will see in these guides are just that; a guide. You should determine a price that you feel comfortable with. Normally I suggest that bidders use a percentage of the published prices when buying at an auction. You should pick a percentage of the published price as your limit. This percentage will change from person to person and from asset to asset, but the premise that guides your bidding should be to get a good deal.

I want my readers to consider two other areas when looking into the value of a car. They are the type of title that is being transferred and if that title is free and clear of any liens. You must consider these factors in your estimate of the asset's value. In some auctions, like the Department of Transportation in both New York and in Los Angeles, cars are sold with the unknown liens. This means that the car you buy at one of these auctions may have a lien on it that will not be disclosed to you and you will be legally responsible for that lien. This can severely impact the apparent value of the car and give you a headache that you don't need. So please be careful and determine if you will get a free and clear title.

I would advise my readers to avoid these auctions due to the potential of hidden problems. In many of these situations the city auctioneer will know if there is a lien on the car and he will not inform the bidders. I find this to be a totally unacceptable practice and object to it strongly. The only way these city departments will change their ways is if the turnout at the auctions drops significantly. You can find lots of other auctions to go to that won't have these surprises.

Just as important as the status of liens on the title is the type of title being transferred. You want a vehicle that you can buy and register quickly. Most states have what is called a salvage title. This is a title that will restrict your ability to register a vehicle until it has been physically inspected by the State Motor Vehicle Department. A car will come to have one of these titles if it was in an accident that caused the insurance company to pay the car off as a total or as a recovered stolen vehicle that might have been stripped, etc. If the car you buy is a repaired wreck and still has a salvage title then you have a big pain in the neck. You will have to make an appointment for an inspection which can take up to two months or more. You must pay a fee for this inspection which is $200 in New Jersey. Then you must have your vehicle towed to the inspection area since it is not registered and not allowed on the road yet. Then you wait and wait. Then you get inspected. Some states require receipts for parts that were reported missing or destroyed on a police report to make sure the replacement parts weren't from a stolen car. God help you if you don't have the required paper work or if you fail the inspection. Then you will have to get the car towed out of the inspection area.

The moral to this story is to determine if your title will be free and clear of liens and easily transferable. I suggest you do not get involved with vehicles with these title problems unless they are a part of your normal business.

BOATS

The appraisal of the value of a boat is more difficult than a car because there are far fewer publications that deal with the marine industry. NADA publishes a guide for boat values which is updated every four months and has an $80 annual subscription price. Aside from the published pricing guides you may try to get an idea of the boat's value by asking boat dealers that handle the brand of boat that is being auctioned if they get a used one of the particular year how much would it cost. Then call another dealer and ask him how much he would pay you for the boat that is being auctioned. This will give you an estimate of the value and if you buy it cheap enough you may have a customer in the dealer you asked to buy it earlier.

Most boat auctions are held at a marina of some sort. You should talk to as many people as possible at the marina until you find someone that may know some of the boat's history. If the auction is a bank repossession auction then it is very probable that the boats were sailed to the marina from the former owners' dock spaces. If you can get some information on how that voyage went you may get some insight on the condition of the boat. Many times boats are sold while they are sitting on land and the condition must then be determined by your visual inspection. It is always nice to know that the boat you are considering will float, but a boat on dry dock will require some careful examination.

I strongly suggest that you hire a professional boat mechanic to come with you to look over the boat you want to bid on. Every mechanic I have brought with me was glad to come because if I bought the boat he was going to get my business to shape up the boat. A boat may be an asset you have desired for some time, but believe me there are a lot of things, expensive things, on a boat that you may not be aware of. So bring someone along to help you not only determine the condition but this person may give you some idea of the value of the boat as well.

I must tell you to be aware that a boat sold by the United States Customs may have some expensive restrictions placed on it. If a boat was used to smuggle drugs into the country, the smugglers may have built hidden compartments to contain the drugs. These hidden and illegal compartments must be removed from the boat to the satisfaction of United States Customs officials. This may become an expensive project that turns a good deal into a bad one.

The Customs service will inform you of any illegal compartments so please read all the information that they provide.

PLANES

If you are in the market for a plane then you will have to get a price guide called the Aircraft Bluebook - PRICE DIGEST. You can contact them at 800-654-6776 or Fax 800-633-6219. They publish 4 issues per year and an annual subscription costs $225. They also have some other specialty publications that will help you get more detailed pricing information on certain classes of aircraft.

This book is widely used in the aviation market place and will give you pricing information on most aircraft. When dealing with aircraft you must employ professional assistance to determine the condition of the craft. Your life may depend on it. Some aircraft that you may encounter may not have logs or records of any kind. Please take every precaution when examining these craft.

The publisher has a policy to only sell his book to "qualified" buyers meaning lenders, manufacturers, dealers, service centers, insurers, government agencies, FAA, tax agencies or consultants. I do not know if this statement is just for publicity or if it is policy so just say you're a consultant or private lender or something appropriate when ordering.

REAL ESTATE

The value of real estate can be determine using several methods. However, when a property is being sold at auction you may not have the luxury of time to thoroughly investigate the value of the property. At most auctions for real estate you will be told that the property was appraised and its value was found to be this or that amount. Many times the dates of these appraisals, if they are disclosed to you, are so old that they are useless. My advice to the real estate buyer is to ignore these appraisals completely. DO NOT RELY ON THEM. Not only could they be out of date, but they could be just plain wrong. The appraisal is only as good as the appraiser. The appraiser that produced this estimate may leave something to be desired. You must rely on your own homework or due diligence.

If you have the opportunity I would suggest hiring your own independent appraiser to assist you. If time constraints prohibit this then try some alternative methods of appraising the property's value. The simplest method is to contact a local realtor and ask them the value of some comparable homes in the neighborhood. Check into the asking prices and the actual discounted prices the properties sold for. I would not disclose to a realtor that you are trying to buy a house in an area at auction. That slip of the lip may create more competition for you if the realtor tells everybody on earth about this house to be sold at auction. If the realtor already knows about the house that is going to be auctioned, you may find him reluctant to tell you about it. The reason for this is that he may not be able to make any money for himself if you buy it, so why tell you. This mercenary attitude may change if the auction protects brokers.

At some real estate auctions the auction sponsor will pay a broker for bringing a buyer to the sale. The range of commission payable to a broker that brings the winning bidder in is normally 2% to 6%. At auctions of this type you will probably encounter realtors at the auction questioning every potential bidder before registration to see if they have a realtor with them. If the bidder does not have a realtor then the realtor will ask to be your realtor in order to get the commission that will be paid on a purchase. Since it will not cost the bidder anything they will ask you. Some realtors will offer to split the commission with you. This type of arrangement could save you money, but it will only be a "hand shake" agreement between you and the realtor. This is a questionable practice, but it does exist and my readers should be aware of it. You will now have more time to consider an offer like this now that you know that it may come your way.

In any event, a realtor can be a valuable source of free information about a property, and I advise you to speak to them. Aside from contacting a realtor you can go to the Town Hall and research any sales in the area around the parcel you are interested in. While you are at the Town Hall you should inquire with the planning board if any development of a negative nature is contemplated. You do not want to buy a house and find that it will be in the shadow of some garbage recycling plant. The potential for adverse development might have been a contributing factor in this property going to auction in the first place.

After you determine the potential value of the property you should determine the condition of the structure. It is very easy and inexpensive to hire a renovation contractor to come and look at the house. He will be able to give you an estimate of the cost of any needed repairs, and you should adjust your bid accordingly. You should also consider insect infestation, lead paint and radon as potential bid lowering items.

Other areas that may be of concern to you are school district quality, and one of my favorite subjects: real estate taxes. You may be surprised to learn that many buyers of real estate at auctions fail to determine the amount of the annual tax bill on the property. Some properties that are sold at auction have back taxes that are due on them. Take the time to investigate this. Do not make the mistake of assuming that the house that is being sold in the same neighborhood as yours will have about the same taxes as your house, especially if the house to be auctioned is newly constructed. Many towns seem to believe it is proper to tax new homes far higher than older homes. I do not know how they can get away with this, but they do. So please determine the tax burden of the house and be especially aware of the dreaded "estimated" taxes. These estimates are never correct and, amazingly, they always seem to underestimate the true final tax bill.

On the subject of TAXES. I would like to conduct a survey of my readers. Please inform me if your tax bill has ever gone down all by itself. This does not include any efforts on your part or your attorney's to get a reduction. I just want to know if there is some place in this great country that may have a sane tax structure. Everything involved with economics has a natural cycle: they go up and down. But real estate taxes just seem to go up and up and up. This steady climb is approaching the breaking point in communities all over this country. Something has to give, and soon.

Too many people are getting hurt by this system and relief and reform are in order. I know a man who lives on Long Island, New York. When he moved their 30 years ago his tax bill was $1,000 per year. This man worked hard for his money his whole life and retired six years ago on a fixed modest income of $17,000 per year. When he retired his tax bill had swelled to $6,200 per year. Today, his tax bill has sky rocketed to $8,900 per year. This amount is eating up over half of his income. And I just heard on the evening news that the county he lives in wants to raise taxes by 20%!!! ARE THESE POLITICIANS OUT OF THEIR MINDS? THEY HAD BETTER CUT THEIR COSTS AND REDUCE SPENDING. Then they always say they will have to reduce services. FINE! If they do not get this system under control they won't have anyone left to provide their services to because no one will be able to afford to live there.

The real estate tax system is running wild like a nuclear reactor heading for a full core melt down. After a while nothing can stop it and you get a catastrophic disaster with many, many people getting hurt. People are people, not money trees with an unending supply. Something must be done and you, the tax payer, has to do it. Well, you didn't buy this book to hear me rant and rave about taxes so I'll get back to the subject of auctions.

An ominous sign of the trouble with taxes is the significant number of houses being sold at auction for tax liens. Contact the local Receiver of Taxes in an area you are interested in and inquire about tax lien auctions. There are many terms and conditions with sales of this type, and they will vary from state to state.

COINS

The coin market is subject to price fluctuations from many factors. Economic conditions, rarity, quality and even the auction house that is doing the selling can effect the value of coins. As with all the other categories I would suggest purchasing a pricing guide for coins to help you determine the prices of a coin. I will list a few publications for you to consider.

One thing these guides will not give you is the "eye" for quality. The value of a coin is highly dependant on its particular quality. What may look perfect to you at an auction may look just average to a dealer. This is an area that will only be perfected with experience. You will be able to get started investing in coins sold at auction with the information these publications provide. They will list almost any coin you may encounter and will give you a good basis of value of the coin.

As I had mentioned, earlier the auction house can affect the prices fetched at auction. If you were to take the identical coin and sell it at a postal auction the price would most probably be significantly lower than if that coin were to be auctioned at Sotheby's. Try to find auctions of coins from unusual sponsors, such as postal or police auctions. The chances of your getting a good deal are greater at these auctions. Many times these auctions will only advertise "assorted coins to be auctioned" and you may be very happy with what you find. The government auctioneer normally will not have a clue to a coin's value. If you are the only one that does know then you have hit the jackpot.

Suggested publications:

The Numismatist
818 N. Cascade Ave.
Colorado Springs, CO 80903

Coinage Magazine
2660 E. Main Street
Ventura, CA 93003

Coin World
P.O. Box 150
Sidney, OH 45365

Coin Magazine
700 East State Street
Iola, WI 54990

Numismatic Coin Weekly
700 East State Street
Iola, WI 54990

Some inexpensive price guides are published by:

Western Publishing Company, Inc
Racine, WI 53404

They publish several books so make sure you get the book that covers the area you are interested in.

ANTIQUES AND COLLECTABLE

In the world of antiques and collectibles a vast number of assets of every imaginable source may be for sale at any time at auction. To help you familiarize yourself with the asset type that interests you I would suggest two initial procedures. First, go to your public library and see what they have on the area you are interested in such as baseball cards, comic books, etc. If you find a useful guide then I would suggest you order it to have it handy.

A popular book for pricing antiques and collectibles is published by:

Crown Publishers, Inc.
225 Park Ave. South
New York, NY 10003
Title: Kovel's Antique and Collectible Price Guide

You should be able to find this in most book stores. You should be aware that this book is upgraded annually and therefore will be of little use when major trends in pricing are developing. Since the price of an antique is largely based on the buyer's perception of value, it is difficult to report on prices in general. If this area is of interest try to keep up with current events in that area with trade publications and the like.

JEWELRY

You will find a large number of auctions that deal with jewelry. The sources of the jewelry may range from probate estate liquidations to seized goods.

The variety of goods will be vast and your opportunity to inspect them may be limited. Jewelry auctions are one of the more difficult ones to determine the value of an item. The reason for this is that each piece has three potential values. One value would consider the components that make up the piece, such as weight of gold or amount of gem stones in the piece. People look at this as the base value with the idea of dismantling the piece and pricing the individual commodities that make it up. A second pricing strategy is to determine the wholesale value of the complete piece that will be sold as is. And the third price strategy would be to consider the retail price. The retail price level is normally considered by people buying for personal consumption.

To gauge the value of a particular piece I would suggest looking at the weight of the precious metals in the piece and pricing it accordingly for "boring" pieces. For pieces that are beautiful and unique I would attach a premium over the weight price. The amount of that premium will vary on your personal taste. But try to compare it with the value of similar items that you might have encountered.

If you can bring an appraiser with you to the auction you will further protect yourself when establishing a price. Especially when you are looking at gem stones, subtle differences in quality will translate to significant differences in price. These differences will not be detectable to the untrained eye, so bring one with you.

BUSINESS ASSETS

Business assets can include anything from paper clips to entire businesses. With the number of bankruptcies and down sizings on the increase you will find opportunities to bid on business assets almost every week. We bought all of our office equipment, from the phone system and filing cabinets to the desks and chairs at auctions. These assets are easy to establish the value of. Simply shop around for the best deal you can get on an item. Discount that price by 35% to take into account the used status of the equipment, and discount the price further based on the condition of the item. For instance, a five draw lateral steel filing cabinet would sell new for about $500. I would price it at $325 to establish a good value. It turned out that I bought these cabinets within a price range of $20 to $75 apiece. Your common sense will help you get a great deal with every day business assets.

To determine the value of a business or a division or a delivery route, I strongly suggest that you retain professional, competent legal and accounting advise. These assets can be extremely complex, with many hidden values and liabilities. Most buyers have an attitude of "bottom fishing" when bidding on assets that are difficult to asses the value of. Try to buy assets of this type at a level that you know you cannot get hurt at.

PART 1

CHAPTER 3

THE AUCTION

The auction is the portion of the auction process where the prices for the assets that are to be sold will be determined. Each asset will be put on the auction "block" and the auctioneer will receive price bids from the participants. (In the past, items were physically put on a block of wood or stone for people to view during the sale. Today only the phrase survives.) Auctions have been in existence from early Greek times, and probably, to a certain extent, even earlier. An auction is a method to determine at what price an item will be sold and who will buy it. There are numerous types of auctions and many segments of each type. This chapter will give you an understanding of the segments of an auction and some of the critical points that you must be aware of. We will also discuss the important personnel involved in the auction.

Normally, the first subject that is addressed from the podium by an auctioneer is the TERMS AND CONDITIONS. This is a segment where the auctioneer will announce the rules of the auction that the participants are expected to follow. In fact the auctioneer is establishing a verbal contract with the auction participants to comply with the terms and conditions set forth. In many auctions this loose verbal contract is put in writing. When you register to participate at an auction you may be required to sign an agreement to abide by the terms and conditions that have been written down. Commonly, these terms and conditions are written on the back of a bidding paddle that you would be required to obtain in order to participate in the auction as a bidder. These paddles have a portion that will record information about the bidder which is retained by the auctioneer to help support the establishment of this contract. The information required about you may be quite extensive, or just your name. Not all auctions require these registrations, but you should be aware that you are agreeing to abide by the terms and conditions written on these documents. The important thing to remember about these written terms and conditions is to READ THEM! Make sure you understand them, and if you do not understand them ask for a clarification.

One of the terms you will commonly see is that all announcements of terms and conditions from the podium just prior to the start of the bidding take precedence over all previous terms and conditions, both verbal and written. This is important for you to realize that what you had previously understood to be the way this auction was going to be conducted may be changed at the last minute. You should pay careful attention when the terms and conditions are announced because they can and will impact the way you conclude your purchase if you are the winning bidder.

This segment of the auction will give you the requirements for payment. The acceptable method of payment and the time requirements for such payment will be established here. It is important to follow these requirements or you may not be able to participate in the auction. If you do not have the required form of payment, i.e. cash, certified check, etc., please do not even attempt to bid. You probably will not have your bid accepted and just cause a delay in the proceedings. I have even seen people asked to leave an auction as a result of this, which can be very embarrassing.

The time requirements for payment must be met or it could result in you losing the opportunity to purchase the asset you bid on. In the event when you have put a deposit on an asset, failure to pay the balance due in the time frame prescribed may result in forfeiture of the asset and loss of your deposit. This is serious, as I have seen it happen dozens of times, but it is completely avoidable by simply following the instructions that were given to you to properly conclude your purchase.

The terms and conditions could contain just about anything you could imagine but some other common subjects that are addressed are title transfer, closing dates, removal requirements, and remedies available to the auctioneer if you default on your payment. Some of the more unusual terms are incorporated in the auctions we perform for the United States Marshal. The winning bidder will be required to sign an affidavit that he or she is not acting on behalf of the criminal or civil defendant in regard to the purchase of the asset that is being sold. If the bidder is buying the asset for the defendant, that is a crime punishable under law with a jail term of up to five years and/or a fine of up to $10,000. As you can see it is very advisable to pay attention to the Terms and Conditions segment of an auction.

Once the terms and conditions have been concluded the auctioneer will start the auction. Depending on the type of auction, which will be discussed in chapters four and five, you will have the opportunity to bid on the assets that are being auctioned. There are many bidding methods, but by far the most popular is the open verbal auction. In this type of auction, an auctioneer verbally sets the bid prices and the bidders normally just agree to the price that the auctioneer is asking for. Many times in these auctions the bidder suggests a bid and the auctioneer may or may not accept that bid. The auctioneer is in complete control of this type of auction.

This brings me to the subject of the auctioneer. The auctioneer has a job to get the maximum dollar value to be bid for the assets he or she has to liquidate. As with all aspects of business there exist good and bad auctioneers. A good auctioneer will make your auction experience a pleasurable one. He will efficiently proceed with the orderly sale of the assets in a professional manner. He will show respect to the bidders and insure the highest level of integrity is maintained. A good auctioneer is a credit to himself and his profession. A bad auctioneer may be a boring, inefficient mess and I hope you never run into one.

Most states have some licensing requirements for auctioneers that establish basic guidelines of behavior. However, an auctioneer is as unique as a performer. His or her personality and approach to the sale of assets is what you will experience at the auction. Some auctioneers will call (announce) the auction in the manner you may see in old time movies, where they talk so fast that you haven't got a clue to what they are saying. Others will call an auction with clear, concise, easily understandable language. The fast talking auctioneer is a vestige from the old South after the civil war but is still popular in many areas. In fact, some schools for auctioneers in the Midwest are attempting to keep this style alive.

In today's society, with our advanced communications and information processing ability, clarity is something we have strived for as a culture. The accurate dissemination of knowledge is what will advance our society into the future. I believe that any actions or practices that inhibit clarity and understanding should be left in the past where they belong. I have been at auctions with the old fast talking auctioneer trying his best not to trip over his own tongue and have seen entire audiences of bidders with dumbfounded looks on their faces. The bidders are there to spend or invest their hard earned money and they should not be confronted with the situation that requires a translator. The auctioneers that practice this method of calling believe that they will get higher prices if they go so fast that people are caught up in the process. Well, I beg to differ. People today are a lot wiser than they were years ago, and most would like to make an informed decision when buying something. Being able to understand the price that is being asked for an asset sure would help in making that decision.

When you are bidding on an asset you must bid in a manner that attracts the attention of the auctioneer. He must recognize that you are responding to the price he is asking for. We have all seen the stereotyped auction bidder in the movies. He is the guy who sits quietly in the audience, wearing a tuxedo, of course, and acknowledges the auctioneer with just a raise of the eyebrow or with a nod of his head. Let me assure you that this should only happen in Hollywood. Even in an auction that is attended by just a few people, I would suggest that you bid in a manner that will get you noticed. I have seen it happen time and time again, when the auctioneer says "sold" someone will say, "Hey, I was still bidding on that." The auctioneer is a human in the middle of a sometimes hectic environment and no auctioneer I know has E.S.P. So make sure he knows of your intentions to bid. Raise your hand, wave your bidders card, yell or jump up and down; but don't lose the opportunity to own an asset you want because you want to imitate Cary Grant.

Some auctions, like the ones we hold, can get rather crowded with six or seven hundred people in attendance. In these circumstances it is obvious to most people that the auctioneer is not watching them intently. He will scan the audience and focus on a bidder that gets his attention. Many times with large auctions bidding assistants are employed by the auctioneer to help him identify bidders. If you find yourself in one of these auctions make sure the bidding assistant is aware of your intentions. Do not be shocked to see this person jump out of his clothes when you accept a bid that the auctioneer wants. His job is to get the auctioneer to recognize and accept your bid.

When dealing with a bidding assistant I want you to be aware that he is NOT the auctioneer. If he does not do a good job and transmit your intentions to the auctioneer in time you may lose the bid when the auctioneer says "sold" to someone else. I always advise people who are bidding on an asset they want not to rely on the bidding assistant alone. If you want the asset I suggest that you also do your best to get yourself noticed.

In our society I find it funny that people are reluctant to stand up if the audience is all seated. I guess it is the same principle that governs our behavior in elevators. I suggest that you make your presence as noticeable and imposing as possible. You may find that you are able to discourage another bidder if they think you are really serious and intent on winning the bid. I remember an auction I attended for some surplus property in New York City where one of the bidders was patiently going back and forth with another bidder. I imagine when the bid started to approach his limit he got motivated and stood up and shouted his bid. Then he turned around to see who was bidding against him. Now I must tell you that this gentleman looked like a prehistoric madman and his intense presence seemed to convince whoever was bidding against him to be quiet. I don't suggest that you act in a manner that may disturb an auction but if your sincere intent is known by the other bidders they just may say, "This guy really wants this thing" and withdraw if they aren't too committed.

In some auctions the bidding assistants have another function. As I mentioned in an earlier chapter, they will urge you to continue bidding. Please remember to stick to your predetermined bid price limit and don't let this practice get you to go over your limit. If you do go over your limit you may regret it. It is better not to buy something than to buy it and think that you have made a mistake.

PART 1

CHAPTER 4

TYPES OF AUCTIONS

There are many different types of auctions, and we categorize auctions by who is the sponsor. The sponsor is an entity that has hired the auctioneer to sell some assets under its control. It is very important for you to know what type of auction you are going to because certain ones are better than others and certain ones should be avoided altogether. We use four major classifications of auction type. They are: Government Auctions, Court Ordered Auctions, Secured Party Auctions and Private Enterprise Auctions. We will discuss these in depth in this chapter and give you some insight that would have taken you years to develop.

Sooner or later just about anything you can imagine will come up for auction. The diversity of the assets being sold at auction on any one day is amazing. You will be able to find everything from jet planes and real estate to warehouses filled with diapers, etc. As important as the type of asset is the type of auction. Each sponsor will give the auctioneer a set of instructions that the auctioneer will use as a guideline to conduct the auction. These instructions can and do vary widely and will have an impact on the bidder. In addition the type of auction will give you some information about the asset that is being sold and how it came to be under the control of the sponsor.

We will first look at the largest category of government auctions. In this category you will find the federal government and all of its agencies, state governments with all of their agencies, city governments with all of their agencies and all other local municipalities. All of these will sell certain assets at an auction at some time. One fact that is consistent with all these government auctions is that they are legitimate. The assets that are sold in these auctions have come under control of the sponsor, either by direct ownership such as trucks, police cars, office furniture, real estate, surplus assets, etc., or as the result of some action by the various sponsors such as seizure or confiscation.

If you were just limited to attending auctions in this category you most probably would not mind. The volume of assets that are auctioned from these agencies is tremendous. In later chapters you will find guides to help you identify and contact these agencies. The vast majority of these auctions will sell the assets they have for auction on an absolute basis. An absolute auction means that the assets are sold to the highest bidder regardless of the price. In these cases, if you are the only bidder you can buy an asset for as little as a dollar and those assets might be a car, boat or property. However, in all the years that I've been buying assets at auctions I've never bought a high value asset for such a low price. I have come real close, though.

Just about anyone would take a chance and buy an asset for a couple of dollars, because if you decide against it you can just walk away from your purchase and lose the purchase price. If it is only a few dollars, big deal. The way you may get such a great deal is if you are one of a few people that attend the auction.

In some of these auctions you may find some assets have had a minimum price placed on them. This is the price that the bidding will start at. For the most part these minimum prices are great deals if they sell at that level, and they do commonly. You will not buy a high dollar value asset for a few dollars in these cases, but you will get a great deal. Remember, that is how I bought my house. I had to pay $170,500 for it, I finished the incomplete house and now the house and property appraise at over $1,000,000. My equity in this house is well over $700,000! If I did not attend that auction because I thought the minimum bid would be more in line with the real market for a comparable property, I would have missed out on a great deal. That is why it is important for you to attend auctions for assets that you may think are beyond your reach financially. When the auction starts and the minimum bid is placed, you may be surprised that you can afford the asset.

When you are searching for an auction that has an asset you want, give this type of auction a high priority. These are the types of auctions that you always hear about the excellent values that people got at the sale. In addition, you will find that these auctions are held on a relatively regular basis with similar types of assets offered again and again. As with the auctions that we hold for the United States Marshal, we auction off close to a half million dollars worth of cars on a regular basis. If you want an asset of this type, this type of recurring auction will present you with many opportunities.

These auctions commonly have surprises in them. When we advertise an auction we have an advertising deadline to meet which is 11 days before the auction. At the time the advertisement goes in we will list all the assets that are available for sale on that day. In the time between the advertisement placement and the actual sale many assets can and are added to the list of assets slated for auction. These assets that are added may offer you a special opportunity. Since they were not advertised many people will have no idea that they are being sold. If you are looking for a particular asset and one of these sales is scheduled it may pay for you to pass by and inspect what will be sold that day just in case something interesting has been added. If you can't attend at least call the auctioneer and inquire if any assets have been added to the ones they had advertised.

The second major category of auction type are court ordered auctions. These auctions take place as a direct result of a court order. Most of the federal and state courts have the authority to order an auction but the majority of this type of auction come from the federal bankruptcy courts, probate courts and courts that issue judgments in civil actions. When a judgment is handed down, many times assets seized to satisfy the judgment are sold off. Judgments of foreclosure are by far the most common.

These types of auctions should be high on your priority list of auctions to investigate. When the court orders an asset sold off at auction it is usually ordered to be auctioned on an absolute basis. This means the item will be sold on the auction date to the highest bidder regardless of the price. In court ordered auctions one of the reasons that an asset is sold off on an absolute basis is to meet a time requirement that the court has set for the disposition of the asset. They therefore do not have the luxury to wait for someone to hopefully come along and offer them a higher price sometime in the future.

Court ordered auctions can offer you some of the best deals in all of the auction world, and you should pay special attention to them. In latter chapters we will discuss the courts in more detail, including how to contact them. I have seen assets sold at these auctions for pennies on the dollar. Get in the habit of going to these sales. They are legitimate sources for all types of assets. Just think about it: when a major corporation goes bankrupt all of its assets are sold at a court ordered auction. These auctions may sell the company as a whole or sell its divisions separately or even sell off each and every asset individually right down to the paper clips. Some of these sales include hundreds of millions of dollars of assets. The way the company is disposed of is at the discretion of the judge or a court ordered trustee. This is the reason why court ordered auctions are of all shapes and sizes.

The third type of auction is the "secured party auction". This is an auction that private enterprise has ordered the disposition of an asset that was pledged as security to support a debt. The property contractually becomes the property of the secured party when the debtor does not meet an obligation. Since the auction sponsor is having the auction in an attempt to recoup the amount of the debt that the asset was pledged as security for, these auctions are more likely to have a minimum bid or a reserve imposed on it. The minimum bid is the lowest price that will be accepted for the asset and is normally the opening bid. A reserve is when the bidding is allowed to open up and progress. If the bid does not reach a certain level, the reserve, then the asset will not be sold. Normally you will not be told the reserve amount. You can read more about reserves in Chapter 6.

You can find almost any type of asset at auctions of this type. The problem with them is that they are hit or miss situations. The assets will vary and the frequency of such sales is unpredictable. When you do come across a secured party auction take an extra step to investigate the circumstances behind the sale and if the asset is something that has a title. Find out how the title will be transferred and if it guaranteed to be free and clear. The last thing you want is the headache of discovering the asset you had purchased has liens all over it.

The fourth and final auction type is the "private enterprise auction". These are common, and assets of all types are sold at these auctions. The sponsors of these auctions are individuals and companies that wish to liquidate something. The sponsors can be the owner of a baseball card collection or a major corporation looking to sell off some surplus office equipment. In this category you can find just about any type of asset for sale, and certain areas are gaining in popularity. The sale of real estate through auctions is growing quickly in the United States. Currently about 30% of all real estate is being sold through auctions. In Australia almost 90% of its real estate is sold through auctions. An auction gives the seller a quick way to liquidate an asset with limited expense. The seller can protect their interests by putting a reserve or minimum bid on the asset so that if it does not fetch their price they still own it.

There are thousands of auction houses and auctioneers that will handle these auctions. You can find auction houses such as Sotheby's and Christie's handling the finest items on earth to a local auctioneer that handles estates and every day items. In this category of auctions you will find the auctioneer will specialize in a segment of the market such as art, antiques, estates or collections. This specialization will be one way for you to find the assets that interest you. Just focus on the auction houses that handle what you are looking for.

I would like to give you a note of caution when dealing with this category of auction. The potential for fraud and misrepresentation exists in this category and in the "secured party" category. Since the incentive for having some of these auctions is to recoup a loss or to avert some financial problem the motive to defraud exists. When greed or survival are factors in a decision for a private entity to sell an asset, the seller may bend every rule in the book to get out of a bad situation. If they are able to team up with an unscrupulous auctioneer then you must be careful. Read my comments about con jobs in Chapter 1 and remember that you must protect yourself in these situations.

When dealing with the first two categories of government and court ordered sales, fraud is highly unlikely. I suggest though that you pay careful attention to all details of the auction. In my experience, people have the most problems with payment terms or scheduled deadlines. Sixty percent of the problems that are brought to my attention deal with payment, so please pay attention and your dealings with these categories should be trouble free.

PART 1

CHAPTER 5

METHODS OF BIDDING

If you want something that is being sold at an auction you will have to bid for it. This sounds relatively simple, but there are definite do's and don'ts when bidding. The very idea of putting your hand up and acknowledging the auctioneers price may frighten some people. Especially if you are a newcomer to the auction environment, the hectic unfamiliar pace may make you a little uncomfortable. Let me assure you that there is nothing to be afraid of. Everyone in the crowd is in the same boat as you are. They have all attended the auction with the hope of being the winning bidder for some asset. Everyone in attendance must bid the exact same way you do, so you have plenty of company. I know that you may think the entire auction will have a hush come over it and everyone will turn to see who made that bid just like in the old western when the bad guy comes into the saloon. But that won't happen! Your bid will be acknowledged by the auctioneer and one second latter he will be looking for another bidder to accept his next price. Bidding in an auction will not give you the 15 minutes of fame that we all can expect, just a few seconds.

Now that we have established that there is nothing to be afraid of at an auction, we will discuss how to bid. First thing that you should remember is that as a result of reading this book you have an advantage over someone who didn't read it. Now don't assume that in your first few auctions you will be able to go head to head with a seasoned professional auction buyer, but you will be far ahead of a novice.

At each auction the auctioneer will give you instructions on how to physically bid during the Terms and Conditions segment. Depending on the type of auction, there can be several variations of how to bid, which we discuss later. We will focus our discussion on the most popular method of bidding in this country, the open verbal auction. In these auctions, the auctioneer asks for a price and the bidder will acknowledge that request by either raising one's hand or bidding card or by verbally stating your intention. The strategy of what and when to bid is the important part.

Some bidders swear that the best way to bid is to be in the midst of the bidding right from the opening bid. This, they say, will establish a "strong presence" and help to deter weaker bidders. Other bidders swear the best way to bid is to wait until the bidding slows down to a few players and then loudly enter into the bidding as a new bidder, thereby demoralizing the other tired bidders. These are just two theories on the strategy of bidding that I term "crowd warfare". Whether they are valid is unimportant. What is important is that theories like these, and there are dozens of variations, will help you feel more comfortable at the auction if you happen to adopt one of them.

Aside from these theories I will suggest some strategies that will give you an edge when bidding. The first thing to do is to try and bid in the smallest increments you can. This is something that will be resisted by the auctioneer since it will cost him in time to get the prices to the level he would like to see. He knows that the more drawn out the bidding is, the more time the bidders have to think about what they are doing and withdraw from the bidding. The auctioneer will probably ignore you when there are many bidders hitting his bid, but when the bidding slows down he may be inclined to accept a modest bid advance than the one he was asking for. Get in the habit of using half bids when responding to the auctioneer. For example when he asks for a $100 increase wave your hand or bid card from side to side to signal $50 bid. This will help you save money if the auctioneer lets you get away with it.

When you are bidding, make sure you have the auctioneer's or bid assistants' attention because the best strategy in the world will not work if nobody sees you. The technique you choose for when and how long to bid will be your decision based on what makes you comfortable. What is more important is what to avoid when bidding. There are several tricks of the trade that help the auctioneer get the price up. Do not take it personal, this is his job. But if you are aware of these techniques you can save some money.

One of the more confusing things about a verbal open auction is understanding what price the auctioneer has and what price he is looking for. This is especially true with one of those fast talking, can't-understand-a-word-he's-saying auctioneers. I will give an example of how it may sound: I have $100. Now 2, now 2, now 2. Now $300. If you look carefully at this, the auction started with a $100 bid, then he was asking for two hundred repeatedly. If at this point you keep hearing $200, $200, you may assume he has $200 and offer $300 when he was really looking for $200. When the auctioneer is announcing a number such as $200 I want you to assume that that is the price he is ASKING FOR! Only when the auctioneer speaks clearly and states that he has $200, then you can offer a higher bid. Just please be attentive when listening to the call of the bids. I don't want any of my readers to pay more for an asset than you should because of a simple mistake.

A very important and simple method is often overlooked by all auction buyers, even the professionals. If you are bidding on an asset and you lose the bid, DO NOT LEAVE the auction until the sale of the asset is confirmed. In almost every auction I have ever attended some assets that were supposedly sold came back to the auction block because of some problem with the winning bidder. The problem could be that the bidder didn't have enough money or that he withdrew his bid or just about anything that would cause the sale not to go through.

Now when this asset is put back on the auction block at a later time, it is out of sequence and many of the bidders that participated in the original round of bidding might have left or may not being paying attention to realize that the asset is being offered again. The auctioneer will undoubtedly say, "Lot #33 had sold a few minutes ago for $5,000. I am putting it up for auction again. Will someone give me $5,000?" At this point DO NOT BID at that level. The item only reached $5,000 because the old winning bidder had brought it up to that price. The old winning might have been in a one-on-one bidding battle from the $4,000 level. So since he is out of the bidding it should sell for $4,000. Now you understand why it is important not to jump in at the old selling price. Strange as it may seem, you may see an item that is put back on the auction block sell for more than the price it fetched on the first sale.

Another method commonly used by the auctioneer is called "with the privilege". This method is used when the auctioneer is selling an asset and there are several identical items for sale. For instance, suppose you were at a business termination auction and they had ten filing cabinets for sale. The auctioneer will put one cabinet up for sale and say, "I will sell this with the privilege which will give the high bidder the option to take as many as he wants at the winning bid price." This option generally will work against you if you decide to exercise your option and take all the items at the high bid price. You should only take one! The reason for this is that you were the high bidder which means that no one else was willing to pay as much as you for the cabinet. Let's assume you paid $500 for the first one and the second bidder was at $450; you should be able to buy the second cabinet for between $450 and $500 if all remains the same with the other bidders. As the auctioneer puts more cabinets on the block the price should continue to drop.

I was at an auction of a major firm that had hundreds of five draw lateral files. In this case there was an enormous quantity. I did not bid on the first few batches which were selling for about $150 each, and some people were using the privilege to take 10 at a time. When I started to bid all the high dollar bidders had bought all they needed so I had very little competition. The first one I bought for $75; the next one for $60 all the way down to $20 at which point I bought 10 of them using the privilege.

As a rule of thumb, do not exercise the privilege if there is a huge quantity. Do not exercise the privilege on the first item being sold. You will probably get the second and the third cheaper. If you are buying something that you need a set of, such as an end table, then you should use the privilege. And, finally, if you buy the first one for a great deal then use the option to take as many as you need because you never know if the crowd is going to wake up and start bidding. Buying with the privilege is a little tricky, but you can do well by using your common sense.

At a sealed bid auction you must submit your bid in writing in private. This is a major disadvantage for the bidder because you have no idea of what your competition is doing. The winning bidder on a sealed bid auction may very well be significantly higher than the runner ups bid. You can't just better your competitors' bids by a few dollars as you can in a verbal open auction. In fact, you can't change your bid at all. You have one opportunity to place a bid, and that is it. In these circumstances, you must do some soul searching. First of all establish your bid price limit and then you should make the hard decision as to what percentage of your limit you will write down. It is definitely a tough call to make, but there is no easy way out.

A spot bid auction is a variation of a sealed bid auction with the exception that your written sealed bids are given to an auctioneer that will open them during the auction and sell the asset to the highest bidder. You get only one chance to bid and you have no idea what your competition is doing. These auctions are used very infrequently.

Another unusual auction is the Dutch auction. This method of auctioning is popular in Holland for the sale of flowers. It is an open verbal auction with one significant variation. The bidding at these auctions goes backwards from a high starting price to the eventual lower sale price. The way it works is that the auctioneer will start the bidding by saying $1,000. If no one says they will take it then he will say $900 and keep dropping his price until the first bidder says he will take the bid, and then he is the winning bidder. This type of auction gets interesting when the price drops to the range of a real bargain. Everyone is ready to jump in and claim the asset, but they all will wait till the last second. Once the first bidder accepts the auctioneer's bid, it is over. No one can better his bid. This auction has a potential for favoritism since the winning bidder is the one who accepts the auctioneer's price first. It would be easy for an auctioneer to look the other way to a friend of his for a second and give him the sale. You probably will not come across this auction in America.

As we progress technologically you will see more and more telecommunication-type auctions. These auctions are conducted like a verbal open auction but the bidders are not in the auction house. They are linked to the auction by telephone and can bid and buy from anywhere in the world. These types of auctions deal primarily with high ticket assets, but I believe they will rise in popularity. The bid registration is important at any auction. It is a formality that will enable you to bid. With tele-auctions, the registration process is more detailed due to the long distance nature of the transaction.

I must caution you about bid rigging. Bid rigging is when two or more parties conspire to keep the bid prices down. This is a felony that carries some heavy fines and/or imprisonment. Don't do it!

PART 1

CHAPTER 6

Bidding Methods Chosen By The Auctioneer

Absolute Auction: The Absolute Auction is the best auction to attend because the item being sold (the lot) is to be sold regardless of price. Yes, that means if a home is being sold absolutely and no one else is there except you, you can buy it for $1.00. In all my years as an auctioneer and participant of auctions I have never seen that happen. Low prices yes, giveaways NO. If only a very few people show up at an auction for a very valuable asset, the auctioneer has the right to cancel the sale and re-schedule it again. I remember at one of our sales a man read the advertisement wrong and came to the auction sight one day in advance. This man flew in from down south somewhere and came into the auction sight all psyched up. When I told him the auction was the next day he said, "Damn, I thought I was gonna get me a real swell deal." He came back the next day and bought a nice car for well under wholesale.

Absolute Auctions are not as plentiful as other auctions because they are usually distress sales. In most government sales, the government wants to liquidate their properties quickly because it is in their best interest. When the U.S. Marshal sells seized assets, the profits go back into their anti-crime budget and we all benefit. This makes the Absolute Auction the perfect means of liquidation.

Some of the unscrupulous auctioneers mentioned earlier represent that they will hold an Absolute Auction but have no intention to sell anything for less than their predetermined minimum price. There are a few ways you will be able to figure out which auctioneers are unscrupulous. If you see the same auctioneer selling IDENTICAL items at different locations fairly close in time to their last sale, beware. You will find auctions every week for similar items, but the exact same asset at an absolute auction is very doubtful. Another way is if you see the same items being sold over and over again. If you ask the auctioneer about it and they answer you with some story about the person who bought it at the last sale never picked it up, beware. This may be true but when the same item is there again at their next sale, next time stay home.

Most of the main Absolute Auctions are conducted for the IRS, U.S. Marshal, U.S. Customs Service, INS, GSA, the U.S. Postal Service or are Court ordered. Other common Absolute Auctions are bankruptcy sales, fire sales, flood sales, certain estate or probate sales and some business liquidations. In summary, anything can be sold at an Absolute Auction, and it must be sold regardless of price.

Reserve Bid: A Reserve Bid method of sale is when the auctioneer is directed by the property owner to sell the asset if it reaches at least a minimum price. The auctioneer will usually start the auction and state the property that is about to be sold is subject to a reserve. Most auctioneers will not state what the reserve minimum bid is because they do not want to discourage anyone from bidding higher than the reserve price. Don't be afraid of this type of sale because most auctioneers will not waste their time if the owner of the property is not willing to sell the asset at a reasonable auction price. The auction will begin and the auctioneer will ask for a starting price usually less than the reserve bid. The auction will conclude and the highest bidder will be told if they are successful. At that time, if the reserve was not reached, the seller may choose to accept the highest bid or you can increase your bid to meet the reserve. There is nothing wrong with increasing your bid as long as you are not going past your predetermined maximum bid. It has been my experience that the two parties will come to an agreed price rather than not having a sale.

Most auto repossession sales are handled in this manner. Many times the bank will state they want a certain price or there will be no sale. As the auction progresses they will indicate to the auctioneer whether they will sell the asset for the highest bid price. From that point on the sale becomes an Absolute sale. Their logic is that since the sale is known to be a Reserve sale and the bidding seems to be slowing and the reserve price has almost been reached, if the auctioneer announces the sale is now going to be absolute the bidders will raise their bids. Most of the time this strategy works for the seller because the bidders know they are going to get the asset. Again, always keep to your predetermined maximum bid.

Minimum Bid: This method of sale is similar to a Reserve Bid, only the Minimum accepted price is advertised. If the minimum price is not met or exceeded there is NO sale. This method is usually successful because the minimum price, in most cases, is far less than the property is worth. I have seen houses that started with a minimum price of $50,000.00 eventually sell for $500,000.00, which was still a good deal because the house was worth around $700,000. Most real estate foreclosures use this method.

Upset Price: This is the opening bid the auctioneer requires. The auctioneer determines this opening price, and, in most auctions, it is usually what the auctioneer feels is a fair price. The reason most auctioneers do not start at a lower dollar amount is time. In most auctions there are many properties to be sold, so, in order not to spend all day on one item, a fair starting price is asked for. If the asked price is not responded to, the auctioneer, at his discretion, can ask for a lower upset price or pass the item and move on. If an auctioneer is getting a flat fee for conducting the auction the tendency to pass an item may be greater.

No Reserve Auction: A No Reserve Auction is similar to a Reserve Auction with one important difference and that is the property being sold does not have to be sold for a reserve price. Some items may sell and some may be passed. This type of sale is subject to the owners confirmation. The sale or no sale decision depends on the mood of the seller at the time of knockdown. If the seller feels the highest bid price is fair, then he will OK or confirm the sale. If the seller feels he is giving his property away, then he will not accept the highest bid and a NO SALE will be announced. This type of auction is the most abused by rip-off artists who want to sell their property for retail prices. If they do not get a retail or almost retail price they refuse the sale. This becomes a waste of the auctioneer's time as well as yours.

Secured Sale: A Secured Auction Sale is nothing more than an auction being conducted for any seller for any reason. This type of auction rarely sells anything at a great price. The use of the word "Secured" in the advertising of the sale is used mostly to try to mislead you into thinking there is a forced sale circumstance when, in fact, there may be none. These sales often sell broken or outdated items, so unless you know the auctioneer's reputation try to avoid them.

Watch out for advertisements with come-on phrases like "Going Out For Business" or "To Avoid Bankruptcy". These play on words can cost you. Also remember that some forced sale auctions are only forced sales because the seller bought the property to sell for a profit and not to keep for themselves. If you see any of these types of sales I strongly suggest that you call the auction company and ask as many questions about the sale as you can. If you're not satisfied with the answers, stay home.

PART 1

CHAPTER 7

Open To The Public

General Admission: General Admission is exactly that. Anyone may attend. However, only persons of legal age and with money may bid. Many people think auctions are for dealers only, and you can bet the dealers who are looking to buy wish that were true. The fact is most auctions today are open to the public.

Trade Restriction: This type of sale is open only to persons of the same trade. The sale of tobacco is one case when the general public is not allowed to attend. The reasoning for trade restrictions is simple: why have people around who have no intention of buying anything. Another reason is that this type of auction has special terms and conditions that are normal and expected of persons in the trade. In order to avoid unnecessary legal problems, only professionals of the trade are allowed to attend. Still another reason is because the trade participants are acquainted with the auctioneer's methods. The auctioneer may speak very fast, and most of the general public would not understand anyway, so only trade people may attend.

Some of the types of trade restriction auctions are: large machinery, raw gems, jewelry, salvage yards, electric components parts, raw materials, drugs and alcohol, to name a few. Anything that is not normally available to the public may be auctioned by trade restriction.

Many times, assets that are to be sold in bulk or for wholesale are sold with trade restrictions. Cars and household items are often sold this way. I cannot understand the logic of the sellers since an auction that is open to the general public will usually bring a higher return for the seller.

Financial Restriction: As you know, a vast amount of high priced properties are sold through auction. In order to insure that serious bidders attend, a financial restriction is put on. This restriction varies from auction to auction. This restriction is usually in the form of a cash or certified check deposit which is collected before you may be admitted to the auction. If you are not the successful bidder, or if you decide to leave early, your deposit is refunded. If you are the lucky bidder your deposit will go towards the purchase price. If your deposit is greater than your purchase the balance will be returned if you paid it in cash. If you paid by certified check the difference will be refunded once your check has cleared. On higher priced assets a 10% deposit is usually required, but it can be more or less, depending on the auctioneer. On lower priced assets $100.00 is the most common restriction deposit. Again, this deposit can vary.

If you are the successful bidder and fail to comply with the terms and conditions, your deposit will be forfeited. Please do not forget you gave a deposit because that deposit is not refundable once you are the successful bidder. The whole idea of financial restriction is so the auctioneer will not have to resell the asset because the bidder was a dead beat. I have seen people get "buyer's remorse" and ask for their deposit back, but as in all auctions they must pay the remaining balance or lose their deposit. I have heard all kinds of stories on why the successful bidder should get their deposit back, but have never refunded a deposit unless there was a mistake on my part or the asset somehow was damaged after the sale.

PART 1

CHAPTER 8

Paying For Your Purchase

Available Mortgages from the Seller: Many times, when selling real estate, in an effort to attract more customers and get the highest price possible through an auction, the seller may give a mortgage to a qualified bidder. Your deposit will usually not be refunded if you do not qualify. You will also be required to close or lose your deposit. In most cases the qualifications are minimal, but be careful! Make sure you call the auction company or the seller to find out if you will qualify. You certainly do not want to put your deposit down unless you are assured of getting the mortgage. I have seen only a very few mortgages given without any qualifications, and these were properties most people would not want.

Pre-Qualifying for a Mortgage: To do this you must contact the seller or a private lender (Bank or Mortgage Company) and submit the information they need to pre-qualify you for the maximum amount you wish to borrow. To get a mortgage for auctioned property is usually pretty easy since the lender realizes the property should be sold well below the retail price. Since there is enough equity in your purchase the approval comes much easier than the typical retail sale.

Many lenders will not even inspect the property and will base their approval on your ability to repay. Here is where great credit comes in handy. Because most auctions are in a "time is of the essence" situation, if you are going to a private lender they will have to get your approval quickly. You will have to shop around for this service. To find a lender who will give you a good mortgage rate and quick service isn't easy. Unfortunately most Real-Estate auctions do not offer mortgage money. However, most of the larger auctions and government sales do.

Use of Home Owner Equity: If you own a home and have some equity in your home you can use that equity to get the mortgage money needed to buy the new auctioned property. If you do not have much equity, whatever you do have will help pre-qualify you for the new mortgage. Lenders love good payers and refuse bad or late payers. I always feel if you have equity in your home you should use it to make money. With interest rates and Real-Estate appreciation low, you can do much better investing your equity. Always keep your head at an auction, and if you are intending to sell for profit, make sure you know what you need to earn to be better off than if you just left your equity alone. Remember, there are taxes and other closing costs that take some of your profit or equity.

Establish a Line Of Credit: This is one of the best things you can do if you are able. I just mentioned one of the best ways to do this and that is with your home equity. By having a line of credit, you have a pre-approved source of money should you need it for any reason. Once you have a line of credit you just write a check and the money is available. Some credit line lenders may ask for continued proof of employment from time to time. I suggest that even if you have no plans to use your credit line get one because you never know what may come your way that requires extra money.

Charge Cards: Pros - Having charge card credit is almost a necessity in today's world. More and more people and businesses do not want to use cash. If you are able to pay off the cards every month you will not have to pay interest. Here again you can get credit cards to give you the extra cash you might need to buy something at auction that is a great deal. The longer you have a credit card and you have established that you are a good payer, the easier you will find getting a mortgage or more credit.

Cons - The biggest problem with credit cards is no self control. Americans love to charge, but fail to realize they have to pay for what they buy. Credit Card interest is the other main problem. I often wonder if someone offered to sell you something but told you you must pay 12 to 20 percent interest on your purchase until it was paid off, would you do it? Another problem is if you do not pay your credit card on time, or not at all, your credit report will be damaged for seven years. Seven years is the time bad credit history may stay on your report. Seven years is a long time. A few simple late payments can get you rejected for a home mortgage.

Negotiating Stated Terms: Most of the time you must live with the stated requirements in the Terms and Conditions of the sale. However, as in almost everything, there are exceptions. You may be able to get some concessions of some sort. In very large bankruptcies, because the willing buyers are few, the stated terms may be altered to attract a buyer. When an expensive yacht or ship is being sold "where is, as is" and the engines are not started, the seller may allow the buyer the right to have the engines checked out to see if they run before final payment is made. If you are a little short on your deposit the auctioneer may allow the smaller deposit, if you are lucky. You may be able to stretch the closing or final payment if the seller is reasonable.

My best recommendation to you is to be fully prepared to comply with all the Terms and Conditions before you attend a sale. Never rely on your hope to negotiate stated terms.

PART 1

CHAPTER 9

Concluding Your Purchase

Real Estate Closing: Auctioned real properties with no contingency for a mortgage and delivered free and clear are simple. You can even close without an attorney if you wish, but I suggest you have one with you unless you are purchasing from the government. Even then you may still be better off getting an attorney. At the closing you bring the certified funds needed to close and sign the necessary papers, and you're done. If a problem comes up on the title, like a lien, the seller is responsible to pay it off or clear it up.

Most of the Real-Estate sold is sold free and clear, but if it is not, make sure you instruct your attorney to order a title search for you. If the title report shows a clear and lien free title, get title insurance. Every once in a while a title report shows no liens on a property and you assume the property is free and clear only to find out after you close that a lien has surfaced. By getting title insurance, the insurance company has to pay any undetected liens. There can be liens or second mortgages on the property that can change a good deal into a disaster.

I attended a foreclosure auction which had a first mortgage on the property of $400,000.00 to see if the property would sell. The court appointed referee at the sale announced there were liens and a second mortgage on that property for more than $1,000,000.00 which had to be satisfied. In case you're wondering, no one bid because the liens were far more than the property was worth. If someone came late to the auction and did not hear about the outstanding liens or did not find out about them before the auction, as I did, they would have gotten themselves into real trouble.

If the property is contingent on your obtaining a mortgage, get ready for an experience you will not forget. The lender will ask you more question than you can believe and make you sign more papers than you would ever expect. As unnecessary as it may seem, that is the way it is done. You will definitely need an attorney because the lender will require you to have one. If, for some reason, you are not given a mortgage, your deposit will be refunded.

In most auctions that have mortgage contingencies the seller usually will have pre-approval terms. If you do not get approved before the sale you must pay for the property in full yourself. If you attempt to buy the property and cannot come up with the money to close you may lose your deposit.

I attended a bankruptcy sale with twelve individual lots that sold first individually and then in bulk. Property is usually sold first in bulk and then in lots. The bulk buyer sat back and added up what everyone paid per lot and then bid a little more than everyone and got the entire piece. He put down $250,000.00, but was unable to get financing and, unfortunately, lost his deposit. Financing was available but he did not pre-qualify. I found out he hoped to flip the property (sell the property within a few days) to a prominent builder and make a nice quick profit. His brain storm cost him $250,000. The property was sold a few months later to the builder that the poor loser offered to flip the property to. Never buy unless you know you will be able to close!

Change In Asset Condition: One of the most common problems with buying auctioned assets is damage after your purchase. For some reason items disappear or are damaged before you take possession. If this should happen, it is the seller's obligation, not the auctioneer's, to deliver the asset in the condition it was in when you bought it. If, for example, you buy a home and there is a break-in or storm damage or anything else that changes the value before you take possession, you can negotiate the damage repairs or get your deposit refunded. Most of the time the seller will be agreeable to taking off money and be done with the sale rather than refund your deposit, incur handling costs and be burdened with trying to resell at another auction. If something is missing or minor damage occurs it is very difficult to prove the asset is not in its sale condition. To avoid this situation always take possession as soon as possible. If at all possible, take a photo of the asset you bought during the sale.

Change In Material Fact: This is when the auctioneer represents an asset to be one thing and it turns out to be another. We once sold a car that was made to look like a much more expensive model. The correct model information was announced several times but the person who bought the asset did not let that information temper his bid. He paid more than that actual model should bring in with the alterations but paid less than the more expensive model would have brought. If I did not announce the asset was the actual model then that would have been a change in material fact and the sale would be improper. If this should happen, and it sometimes does, you have the right to cancel your purchase. In all our years as auctioneers I am proud to say we have never had to deal with a change in material fact. Before our firm sells anything we make sure we know exactly what we are selling. However, some other firms may not be as diligent as we are, so you must be aware of this possibility.

Payment: This is the most important part of your Terms and Conditions. As mentioned earlier it is vitally important to understand how you must pay. I say it over and over again, it is printed on the auction paddles and the method of payment is stated in the advertisement but people still get it wrong. Most auctions require cash, certified check or official bank check. If you bring any other form of payment you may not be able to return in time with the proper funds and you may lose your deposit. The reason most auctioneers only accept these type of checks is because they are almost impossible to have a stop payment put on them. This virtually eliminates all the problems that can come up with accepting normal personal checks or credit cards. We have a cash or certified check requirement on the day of sale only. After the day of sale we only accept certified checks and no other form of payment is permitted. A man came in from out of state and only brought money orders to pay, which we do not accept. He not only had the wrong form of payment but he came the last day before the pickup deadline. He tried to have a local bank help him but was unable to obtain the proper funds so he forfeited his deposit.

I strongly suggest you pay very close attention to the final pickup and removal time limitations part of the Terms and Conditions. You can lose you deposit or even lose your fully paid for asset if they are left past the allowed time. You may go back to the location of the auction and find a new business there who disposed of your property. If this happens you're just out of luck.

Titles of Ownership: When you buy seized government automobiles or boats you will receive a lien free government title which allows you to go to any state and obtain a new state title. If you are buying from an auto or boat wholesale auction you will receive a transfer form from them which allows you to obtain a new state title. Make sure you understand the Terms and Conditions pertaining to who is responsible if any liens are present. I strongly suggest you only buy when the asset is offered free and clear.

Real-Estate Titles or Deeds are delivered the same way they are if they were not auctioned, only the time for closing may be shorter. You simply show up, pay your balance with the proper funds and you are issued a title or deed.

For any personal assets that are sold, your sale receipt is your proof of ownership and no form of title is given. Buying personal property at auction is the same as buying in a store, only it should cost you less.

Right of Seller to Withdraw Asset: At any time before any sale, whether it is an Absolute sale or not, the seller has the right to withdraw all or some of the assets that are to be sold. There are times before an auction starts that the owner decides to keep an asset or sell it to someone without letting it go to the auction block. Fortunately this does not happen too often. Most auctioneers will not participate in a sale in which the seller may withdraw the assets.

Liens: Liens can be on any asset that is available for auction. Liens can be in the form of unpaid business bank loans with all the remaining assets of the company held to satisfy the unpaid balance. Liens can also be many individual actions to recoup moneys owed.

Mechanics Liens: Mechanics Liens are some of the most common. These occur when someone is hired and not paid for their labor. Once a lien is put on a property, that property has a permanent legal action attached to it. Unless the lien is satisfied it stays with the property and can be acted upon if the lien holder feels he can recover his loses.

Any time an asset is being purchased with a lender's money, the lender will usually demand any liens be satisfied. This demand is most common in real estate sales. If you are buying anything without a loan you can buy the property subject to the existing liens. Since most people want their money most liens are negotiable.

Mortgages are a form of lien. You cannot sell your real estate without first paying off your loan. Financing or leasing of a car is another lien. Just try not paying for a while and see what a lien can do. Until a lien is paid off the lien holder is joint-owner with you and can act to have the property sold if you do not pay as agreed.

Another big lien holder is our Tax department, the Internal Revenue Service. These liens can really cost you. In some cases the interest and penalty can be almost as much as the original amount owed. If your taxes are not paid you will have to pay a penalty and interest of over twenty percent on the whole amount owed. The interest due is, of course, compounded. Always pay your taxes first before anything else because you do not want to feel the power of the IRS.

Bankruptcy is one of the only ways to settle a lien without paying it off in full. Let's say your company runs into financial trouble and cannot pay off its creditors. The creditors want their money and they are ready to take you to court. If you go to court, the court will allow them to repossess any remaining inventory you may have and can put a lien on your personal assets if you are not incorporated. If you are incorporated and your company has any other assets they can have a lien put on them. Assets like office furniture, company cars and company owned real estate can have liens put on them. Claiming bankruptcy can stop the repossession and give you some time to reorganize. The creditors can ask the court to order you to have your assets sold at auction, and whatever the court appointed auctioneer recovers from the sale will be the creditors' full payment. Should the auction bring more than the original debt plus court expenses the extra money will go to the troubled business owner. Since most debtors and creditors are fed up with all their problems, they usually do not really care much about the price the assets sell for. As long as they can put this unpleasant experience behind them they are satisfied. This logic makes for a low price auction and usually proves to be so.

Forfeiture of Deposit: One of the main intentions of this book is to save you money. Forfeiture of your deposit is exactly what we hope you will avoid after reading our book. I ask myself why people who work hard for their money would ever allow their deposit to be forfeited, and I come up with two main reasons. One reason is they changed their mind because they realized they paid too much for the asset. As I explained, this commonly happens with Auction Fever. The other reason is they did not understand the Terms and Conditions.

If you do not understand the Terms and Conditions before an auction, I cannot stress enough the importance of getting a clear understanding. Whatever the Terms and Conditions say, you had better be prepared to follow and accept their instructions. As much as the auctioneer may not want you to forfeit your deposit, there may be nothing that can be done. The whole idea of an auction is that the seller wants to liquidate an asset as fast as possible with no strings attached. This is why most auctions sell their assets "where is, as is", in return for which you, the buyer, can save money. If the Terns and Conditions are explained before the auction you have no one to blame but yourself if you do not follow them and forfeit your deposit.

We sold a luxury European car to a lady at one of our U.S. Marshal sales. She was very pleased with the price she paid and couldn't wait to have her husband see the car. She put 20% down as the terms called for and had two business days to pay in full and remove the car. She brought her husband back and he was not happy because he wanted her to buy a six passenger car and this model was only a five passenger. They asked if they could get their deposit returned because they could not use the car. I had the unpleasant job of explaining their deposit was non-refundable. I explained the Terms and Conditions to them and showed them that they were written on all our paddles. They admitted they understood the terms but asked if there was anything I could do. We often get people who, after a sale, wish they had bid up a little higher on an asset so they could have been the successful bidder. Some of these people call to see if anyone does not pick up their property so they may get another chance at an asset. Luckily we found someone who was happy to take over the payment, and they refunded them their deposit. This incident ended happily, but it could have just as easily gone the other way. We were glad to help, but remember that an Auction company is not obligated to do what we did.

After another sale for a Bankruptcy someone called my office and wanted to know when he could pick up the items he bought two weeks earlier. I thought it had to be someone I knew joking around since the removal and payment for that auction was the day of the sale only. It wasn't long before I realized this person was for real. I checked and there were some items not paid for. He then said he figured we would hold the property for him until he was ready for it. Now I figured he had to be a comedian. Unfortunately he was not, so I called the party we conducted the sale for to see if his items were still there. To make a long story short, the landlord took possession of the building and threw everything left in the building away to prepare the building for his new tenant. This person lost his deposit and his items. I said to him if he had called the next day maybe the landlord would have given him his items, but it was out of my hands.

If a person puts a deposit on something and then realizes they really can not afford it, to forfeit the deposit is probably the worst thing they can do. Think about it. You already spent on the average 20 to 25 percent down. I feel you would be much better off paying for the asset and turning around and selling it as quickly as possible. If you paid an average auction price you stand a good chance of making some profit. If you have to, you can always reduce the price to the level you would have lost had you forfeited your deposit. The probability of not finding someone to purchase your asset, especially if you lowered the price, is very slim. Unless you cannot come up with the money to pay for your property, never forfeit your deposit.

Picking Up Your Purchase: Believe it or not, there are some people who pay for their property in full and never pick it up. This does not happen often, but it does happen. Paying for an asset and not picking it up will cause you to forfeit the property. In most retail stores, if you do not return to pick up the property you purchased or put a deposit on within thirty days you will lose the property. In an auction you can loss the property as soon as the Terms and Conditions requirements for pick up are not met. Sometimes you can be charged a storage fee. These fees are usually high in order to deter their use.

As I stated earlier, many times there is only an empty building to go back to after the pickup deadline. We had a man pay $1,500.00 in full for a drug-seized car. The telephone number he wrote down was not working and the deadline for pickup was over. We had his address and, because he spoke very little English, I sent one of my employees to his house to see what happened. My employee was unable to find this man home, so we resold his fully paid for car at our next auction. His lost money went to the U.S. Treasury and he helped reduce our national debt. To this day we never heard from him again. We had another car paid for in full that was never picked up. The person who bought and paid for the car happened to come after inspection was over and never got to see what he was buying. He paid for the car in full instead of leaving the 20% minimum deposit at knock down. When he returned to pick up the car he found the car was in poor condition and walked away disappointed. If he would have read this book he would know, "never buy anything unless you inspect it and set an auction bid price limit".

Some of the assets that are left over or passed at an auction may be resold either through auction at the end of a sale or by a negotiated sale. Here is where you can get the real fantastic deals. It is not uncommon to sell an asset for the balance due of a forfeited sale. Sometimes the seller may unload the asset for even less than the unpaid balance, depending on how much they want to liquidate the asset. Items that are passed usually seem to bring pennies on the dollar. However, if you get too cheap in your bidding the auctioneer may pass the asset and refuse to sell it at that auction.

I have seen passed properties sell for considerably more money than what was expected at the very next sale. This represented a missed opportunity for real savings because no one was interested or aware of the potential savings at the original sale.

Here are some important things to remember when you are picking up your purchase:

1. If you're buying a car make sure the vehicle identification number is correct on your paper work. Too often this mistake causes you to have to return to the auctioneer to have it corrected.

2. If you are paying sales tax be sure you get a receipt for the taxes you paid.

3. Always inspect the property to see that it is what you bought and that it is in the same condition it was in when you bought it. Just because you buy at an auction that states you are buying "where is, as is" does not mean if the property gets damaged or has parts missing after the sale you have to take it. Most auction companies know the condition of the assets they are selling and very few get away with false claims of damage or missing parts after a sale.

4. It is always a good idea to pickup and remove your purchase as soon as you can. This helps eliminate some of the missing parts and damage problems.

5. Make sure you bring the necessary PROPER funds to make final payment.

6. Do not forget your deposit receipt. Without it you have no proof you gave a deposit. A lost receipt should be reported quickly since many auction companies will release an asset to anyone who has a deposit slip and pays the balance.

7. If you are buying a car ask the auction company if they know if the car's battery is good or if they know if the car is in good working order. Many times a battery goes dead and can not be recharged because it sits in the car for too long a period. If that is the case, and you intend to drive the car, you should bring a good battery with you. If the car is not in proper working order you may want to have a tow truck meet you at the auction pick up site.

Taxes: Most auctions have people who attend and buy with the intent to resell the assets they buy. In most states there are sales taxes that have to be collected by the auction company. Unless you have a valid sales tax certificate you will have to pay sales tax. Your sales tax certificate will also have to be in the same field as the property being sold. What this means is that if you are in the clothing business, for example, you will have to pay tax on anything not pertaining to that business. This requirement will vary from state to state.

Any personal use items are subject to sales tax. Another thing many business people do not know is if you have a business with a valid tax number and purchase something in a different state and take delivery in that state your purchase is subject to the sales tax of that state. Your tax certificate is only good in the state in which it is issued.

Buying boats, planes, trucks and cars can be different. In most states the auction company has the choice of either collecting or not collecting sales tax. If sales tax is collected on these assets you will receive a tax receipt to be presented when you register the asset. Most auction companies choose not to collect sales tax on these assets because of all the different tax rates of different areas. Since you pay the sales taxes of where you register the asset it is much easier not to collect the sales tax. You will have to pay the sales tax when and where you register the asset.

Some auctions are for the trade only. To attend this type of sale you will need a proper sales tax certificate to be allowed in. Unless you are known by the auctioneer do not try to attend these auctions without a proper sales tax or business certificate.

Always take into consideration the extra money you will have to spend on sales tax. If you are not in business but want to buy and sell assets on a small scale remember that you will have to pay sales tax on your purchase and income tax on the profit. After figuring in all the taxes and your time, set your maximum predetermined bid to insure meeting your goals.

Keep All Documentation: As remote as it may be, if an auction is conducted and is found to be improper or illegal, the property could be reclaimed by the owner. I have never heard of this happening, but there is an extremely small chance it could happen. Without your documentation you may have no way to prove what you paid. In the highly unlikely event that you should have to release the property you bought, you will need your documentation to retrieve your lost moneys from the auction company and the improper seller.

You will also need your documents to claim ownership. It is good practice to save all receipts and documentation for at least three years.

In a normal situation, as mentioned earlier, loss of your documents can be costly. Someone could use your deposit receipt or, even worse, paid in full receipt and pick up your purchase. Always alert the auction company as soon as possible to lost or stolen documentation.

Another reason to make sure you hold on to all documentation is that some documents, as in Federal titles, are numbered and it takes quite a long time to get new documents reissued. From time to time we have people who lose their titles and have to wait a week or more to get a duplicate. This time can be better spent making and saving money.

The best reason to hold on to your documentation is that you may not be able to have them replaced. You may not be able to find the auction company who sold the asset. The auction company may be from a distant state or country making it to costly to get to their office. I heard of a person who bought an exotic Italian sports car that was supposed to be sold free and clear of all liens. As it turned out, there was a rather large lien on the title that the seller was responsible for. This person could not find his documentation and was unable to recall the name of the auction company which sold him the car. He wound up paying the lien off and losing the money that should have been the seller's obligation. Do yourself a favor and keep all documentation in a safe place.

Bait and Switch: Bait and switch is one of the oldest tricks around. In case you do not know what it is, bait and switch is when you come to buy a certain item that has been advertised and when you get to the sale sight the item you were interested in is not there and another item is offered to you. Usually Bait and Switch happens in retail stores. The retailer will try to convince you the substituted item, which usually cost more, is actually a better and smarter buy. In some cases that may be true, but in most cases the retailer is making a larger profit on the substituted item. This commonly happens in the home electronics retail business, but it can also happen at an auction sale. You see an ad for a certain product that seems too good to be true, and when you get there they are out of stock on that item but have this other item that is, in their opinion, better for you. Sometimes a retailer may actually have the item but will rely on their salesmen's abilities to sway you into the product they want you to buy. If you decide to buy retail (I hate to buy retail) always call up to see if the baited item is in stock. It is also a good idea to check out the item in another store to see what the features of the item are and what the sales person thinks about it.

In an auction sale bait and switch is seldom a problem. If a certain type of item is being sold an unscrupulous auctioneer may advertise a more popular item of the same type and not actually have it. However, in an auction the seller may choose not to sell any item they have without notification. Luckily this does not happen often. I have attended some auction sales that advertised fantastic items with tremendous quantity only to find a bunch of junk. The only way to avoid this is to quickly find out which auctioneers are credable and which are unscrupulous. If an ad seems too good to be true it most likely is.

Part Two

PART 2

CHAPTER 1

THE UNITED STATES MARSHALS SERVICE

The United States Marshals Service (USMS) is one of the oldest law enforcement entities in America. It has a history that is rich in honor, integrity and service. From the old western days to today, the United States Marshal has been the police department of the Federal Government. Their responsibilities have evolved as our country has grown from its early history, and they play an extremely important part in our National Justice system. I am honored to be able to work with the professionals of the United States Marshals Service and think they are doing an excellent job.

Although the Marshals have many responsibilities, we will focus on their activities that will lead to an auction of various types of property. Through the National Asset Seizure and Forfeiture Program (NASAF) and various related laws, the Federal government can seize assets from criminals, usually people involved with drugs in one form or another. Various agencies, such as the Drug Enforcement Agency (DEA), the Federal Bureau of Investigation (FBI), the Alcohol, Tobacco and Firearms (ATF) and the Internal Revenue Service (IRS) can seize assets through NASAF, and they will turn over the assets to the care and custody of the USMS. The IRS also will seize and sell property on their own, but when the case involves money laundering of drug proceeds they will transfer any seized assets to the USMS. Many times the IRS is brought into the investigation by DEA or FBI when they find the currency laws are being violated.

The function of the USMS in regard to all seized property is to act as the custodian of the seized assets while the corresponding legal cases go through the courts. When the defendant is found guilty, then the ownership of the assets are forfeited over to the United States of America. Forfeiture of ownership may occur under certain circumstances prior to a conviction or even a trial. This is a very complicated occurrence with many variations. I will not elaborate on the legal avenues of the National Asset Seizure and Forfeiture Program because it would take up a good portion of this book and be terribly boring. Suffice it to say that these government agencies have the ability to seize all types of assets.

As the custodian of the seized assets the USMS is responsible for the care, custody and disposition of the assets in an organized and efficient manner. The disposition of these assets is what is of interest to my readers. In previous years each USMS district, and there are 93 of them, were able to independently decide how to dispose of an asset. They had the options to sell them themselves using various auction procedures from sealed bids, to open verbal auctions, or they could hire professional auctioneers to handle the disposition. The USMS could even turn over the entire liquidation aspect to another government agency, the General Services Administration (GSA). For various very good reasons fewer and fewer assets are being turned over to GSA for liquidation. The USMS prefers to be in charge of the assets all the way through the liquidations process.

At present, the determination of the liquidation process for the majority of assets is moving from the individual districts to headquarters in Virginia. Although many districts still handle the disposition independently, headquarters increasingly will contract a firm to handle the disposition of certain assets for one or more districts. My firm is the firm that handles assets for the Southern and Eastern districts of New York. Combined, they are the largest in the country. This arrangement gives the liquidation of assets continuity and it makes it easier for the prospective auction buyer to keep track of what is happening. When the disposition of the assets was on a discretionary basis with the districts, you could find any number of potential auctioneers handling the auctioning of assets. Now you only need to pay attention to one firm.

The USMS does not maintain a mailing list, but you can find out who is handling the sales. You can get a list of the firms that are contracted currently, by contacting the USMS. The USMS will change firms on occasion, so you may need to contact the district office repeatedly and if you come up blank there, contact headquarters. You can use the listing found in our quick reference in Part 7 of this book to locate the districts and inquire about the contracted firms.

The types of assets you can come across from the USMS will be anything the defendant may have owned: his personal property; his cars, boats, planes; his real estate; and even any legitimate business establishment the defendant might have owned may be available from the USMS. There are certain assets that the Marshal seems to always have an abundance of, which we discuss below.

CARS

The USMS is an excellent source for cars. A large percentage of the assets the USMS handles are cars. One of the first things a drug dealer does is to go out and buy a symbol of his "success", which is normally a fancy new car. Many of these cars are so fancy their owners and their illegal activities stick out like sore thumbs. We handle cars for the USMS, and I can tell you that you will see everything from bullet-ridden pieces of junk to cars with as little as 27 miles on them. The type of car will be anything from a 1911 Model T to a new Rolls Royce. You will find a great number of every day type cars also.

These cars are normally sold at an open verbal auction and they come with a free and clear Federal title. This title you must bring to your state motor vehicle office to get your own state-issued title. They are sold "AS IS" with absolutely no guarantee. During the inspection period at one of these auctions you will only have a few hours to view these cars, and they are normally not started. So you must temper your bid with the knowledge that you do not really know how the car works, so let the buyer beware. Most of these cars were taken from people on the road, so the odds are that the car works. Some of the auctioneers, if they know, will tell you if the car is working. You should ask the auctioneer if they know anything about the car.

The auctions for vehicles are held on a relatively regular schedule of every six to eight weeks. I will tell you from my experience that many of the cars we sell are bought by car dealers. When some people hear this they think they can't get a good deal because of the dealers. This assumption could not be further from the truth. A dealer will stop bidding right around the wholesale level because he has to resell the car and make some money. The dealer is not the competition you should worry about. Your ability to get a good deal will be hampered by the guy that comes to the auction with a pile of money in his pocket and has no idea what he is doing. So remember to set your bid price limit, and good luck.

BOATS

The USMS will sell boats, but not with any great frequency. We do sell them, but the selection is limited. If you want a boat I suggest trying Customs or

Bank Repossession auctions. Keep your eyes open for a boat that the USMS may have because you may be pleasantly surprised.

When the Marshal sells a boat you will get a free and clear Federal title. The boats are primarily sold at open verbal auctions along with the cars or at auctions held at the boat marina. Some districts will utilize a sealed bid auction for boats. Inspection is normally just a few hours and every boat we have sold was not started because they were in dry dock for a few years. As a boat owner who is looking forward to the second happiest day in a boater's life, I suggest you bring a boat mechanic with you to inspect the boat.

PLANES

The USMS is not a good source for aircraft. They handle them only once in a great while. If you are interested in aircraft, I suggest contacting Customs. They have plenty of aircraft in their custody.

REAL ESTATE

The USMS has extensive property holdings. Most of the property in their custody is liquidated through the use of local Realtors. If a property is not sold through one of these brokers, then it will go to auction. This is a very rare event since the USMS is a flexible, motivated seller. To find out what properties the Marshal has and which broker is handling them WRITE to the real estate forfeiture specialist at the district you are interested in. Include a self-addressed stamped envelope for them to use to respond to you.

JEWELRY

The USMS is a very good source for jewelry. They get all types of things, from watches and diamond rings to gold pieces. Much of the gold jewelry is sold for the penny weight. I have seen diamonds up to ten carats be auctioned for far less than the appraised value. The auctions are held on a regular basis and they commonly have hundreds of lots.

The inspection of the jewelry is very limited. The auctioneer may allow physical contact with the pieces, but he may make you rely on their description. Make sure you do your research on the items you are interested in and set a bid price limit. I find that some people have a bit more difficulty sticking to a bid price limit on an item that glitters or sparkles, so do your best.

BUSINESS ESTABLISHMENTS

The Federal government does confiscate many businesses. Most of them are small, but occasionally a big case will come along and the assets of that company or the entire company could be sold off at an auction. Most of these sales are held in conjunction with some court supervision.

You must examine the potential value of one of these businesses very closely. I strongly suggest that you retain an accountant and an attorney in these manners. The businesses you may encounter will vary from a closed store front type store to an ongoing franchise type business. The USMS will keep a business functioning and preserve the jobs of the employees if the business is legitimate and viable. One such case was a bowling alley that was sold for far less than it would have cost to open one up.

GENERAL MERCHANDISE

The USMS has a good amount of personal property that is often sold, along with the vehicles. This merchandise can be anything from computers, fax machines and portable telephones to the entire contents of a home. These items may not be advertised in full detail due to the large assortment of items and the corresponding cost of advertising such a big list. Instead, you may see an advertisement that will read "assorted general merchandise". If you see this type of ad, call the auctioneer and try to get further details. If that does not work, go to the auction and inspect the merchandise anyway.

The method of sale the USMS utilizes is normally an open verbal auction. They will use a sealed bid auction on occasion. As stated earlier real estate is normally handled through Realtors. These auctions are normally absolute auctions. With certain merchandise the USMS may establish a reserve or a minimum bid, but this is not done frequently.

The auctions the USMS hold are normally open to the general public. I have seen some auctions that have had trade restrictions placed on them. This means you must establish that you or the firm you represent are part of an industry, such as being in the car salvage business, to attend an auction of a car junk yard. This restriction is not a government policy, it may be used at the request of an inexperienced auctioneer. You may also encounter a financial restriction where you must have a certain deposit in order to bid.

All auctions held by the USMS must be advertised at least once in a local paper. This is both good and bad news. It is good because you have the opportunity to read the advertisement and become aware of a pending auction. The bad part is that the selection of the local paper normally lies with the auctioneer. As a result you may not be looking in the correct paper for the advertisement. Continuity would be improved if the advertising were required to be placed in the largest circulation paper for the area. We advertise on a consistent basis in the Sunday New York Times auction section, but other auction firms may advertise in a different paper every time.

The Terms and Conditions of any USMS auction are all similar. You may encounter some variation depending on the assets. In general, you will be guaranteed free and clear title; you must be 18 years old to bid; you will be required to sign an affidavit, if you are the winning bidder, that you are not acting on behalf of the defendant. The payment terms may vary from all cash at knockdown to a small deposit with balance due in a few days.

Please pay special attention to the payment terms and removal terms. These are very important. If you do not follow these terms to the letter you run the chance of forfeiting your deposit.

The best way to contact the USMS district in your area is in writing and inquire which firms may be used to auction property. If you are interested in property, ask for a list of the properties or the brokers that are handling them. Address your inquiry to the Forfeiture Specialist and ask them what papers, if any, they use in publication of sales Do Not Call - you must only write to the USMS.

Once you get in touch with the firm that handles the disposition of the assets, ask to be put on their mailing list. Most firms charge a nominal fee for their mailing list to cover its cost. The more mailing lists you can get on the better are your chances of seeing something coming up for auction that would be of interest to you. Some people may be reluctant to spend the subscription price for a mailing list, but I think that is a costly mistake. If you look at the amount of time you would need to spend scouring the papers every day to catch an advertisement, you would save the cost of the mailing list. You know that time is money. In addition, the cost of missing an auction that may sell something you might have wanted could be high.

PART 2

CHAPTER 2

United States Customs Service

The function of the U.S. Customs Service is to insure that anything entering the United States is legal and any import tax, levy or tariff that is due is paid. This government agency attempts to uphold all the various trade and import restrictions and laws. It is empowered to seize assets and arrest any violators who break the import laws. U.S. Customs has agents at all domestic airports and ship ports. Customs works closely with U.S. Marshals, D.E.A., F.B.I., the Coast Guard and Immigration. Together they seize billions of dollars worth of assets every year.

All types of assets are seized from those who try to smuggle into the U.S. or cannot pay the import duties. The seized assets range from small computer chips to large machinery and everything else you can imagine. Many of the assets are sold to the public through auction. Customs is one of the best sources to buy assets at auction. Most assets are sold through open public auction, but some are sold through sealed bid. If you want a car, boat, plane, yacht, jewelry or general merchandise, Customs will have it for you. Some assets can be bought and used in the U.S. and others must be exported. Still other assets are destroyed. Most of the assets sold through open public auction are sold absolute, regardless of price. I attended a Customs sale and saw a brand new cement mixer valued at about $1,800.00 sell for $250.00. At another sale two Russian sable coats sold for $1,500.00 and were worth about $40,000. Yes, to this day, my wife, never forgave me for not getting them for her.

Believe it or not, some people get the idea to import assets but forget, or just do not know, that they have to pay an import tax, duty or tariff. If they are unable to pay the tax, duty or tariff, or if they fail to declare these assets, they will forfeit the assets. Most of these assets will be eventually auctioned to the public.

Certain people buy assets at Customs auctions that are not allowed in the U.S. When this happens the assets are sold with the stipulation that these assets are for export only. Many people feel that if they buy, let's say, a car at a Customs auction that is not allowed in the U.S., they can somehow alter the car to have it allowed in. Save yourself the trouble and expense. If Customs says it must be exported, it must be exported. If a car or any other asset can be altered to meet U.S. specifications, Customs will inform the potential buyers of this option. Another vast amount of assets that are offered for sale are assets that are seized because someone was trying to smuggle them into the U.S. It is hard to believe that there are so many people trying to smuggle, but it is true. When you go to a Customs auction you will not believe the amount of merchandise Customs collects. I cannot understand why someone would risk losing their assets and have the possibility of going to jail for any reason.

Not only can you purchase all types of assets from Customs, but you can also buy businesses and real estate. If a company is found to be smuggling, or is in the business of selling unlawfully imported goods, the business will be confiscated. These business may be liquidated by auction or negotiated sale. Since most of these illegal business are totally illegal the majority are dissolved and never brought to sale. There are, however, a few that are sold, and usually these businesses sell for a fraction of their worth. If the business or person caught by Customs is found guilty, their real estate or other assets, acquired with illegally gotten gains, can also be seized. Seizure takes place if the real estate was purchased with money made illegally or if the real estate was being used for an illegal purpose. You can get some excellent deals when these properties are liquidated and I strongly suggest that you look into them.

A major portion of Customs seized assets comes from drug trafficking. Because of this, Customs has a very large inventory of cars, boats, trucks, and planes. One of Customs' best tools against drug trafficking is man's best friend, the dog. These specially trained dogs can find hidden drugs that man alone would never be able to detect. I have seen these dogs work and be tested and I would have to say they seem to be foolproof. We had some of these dogs inspect some U.S. Marshal drug seized cars that have hidden compartments. A D.E.A. agent placed some drugs that were wrapped in a way that was not supposed to emit any odor in one of the compartments. We did not let the dog or the dog's trainer see which car the drugs were in and gave them a choice of five cars to search. These hidden compartments were in a place you would never think to look but, with just a few sniffs, the compartment with the drugs was found. Because of these dogs and smart Customs agents, Customs is one of the best sources for all types of assets.

Terms: Cash, certified funds and certain major credit cards are normally the only method of payment accepted. Please make sure you fully understand how and when you must pay for and remove any asset you buy. As in most auctions, you can forfeit your deposit and lose the asset if you do not comply with the terms and conditions. Customs also requires, as mentioned earlier, some assets to be sold for export ONLY! There are cars and boats that have hidden compartments in them that were used in smuggling operations. When these assets are sold the hidden compartments must be dismantled or destroyed by the buyer and at the buyers expense. These alterations must be done before you can get a clear title, and there is usually a time requirement for completion. Depending on the asset the alterations may be very expensive, so understand what you are getting into before you buy. These assets will also have to be reinspected and arranging an inspection may take longer than you expected. I suggest that if you are in a hurry to sell or use assets with these restrictions, do not buy.

If you wish to attend a Customs sale, Customs has contracted with the firm EG&G Dynatrend Incorporated to sell all their assets. Dynatrend maintains a mailing list that you can be placed on for a small fee. This list will give you all the sale locations throughout the country and a brief description of all the assets to be sold. It will, of course, tell you the sale location and when the inspection will take place. Customs seems to prefer having the inspection one day and the sale another, so be aware of dates.

To contact EG&G Dynatrend call 703-351-7880, or write to EG&G Dynaterend, Central Headquarters, 2300 Clarendon Boulevard, Suite 705, Arlington, Virginia 22201. In the event that Customs cancels their contract call the U.S. Customs Service nearest you and ask who is handling their asset liquidations.

PART 2

CHAPTER 3

THE RESOLUTION TRUST CORPORATION

The Resolution Trust Corporation (RTC) was formed as a quasi-governmental agency by an Act of Congress to deal with the Savings and Loan banking crisis. When it was established in 1989 they estimated that it would take about 30 billion taxpayer's dollars to clean up the whole mess. Well, they blew that 30 billion pretty fast and the final cost will probably amaze and depress just about anyone. This banking crisis just keeps rolling along with a seemingly never ending supply of thrifts going insolvent. Now we are hearing rumblings about some big commercial banks.

The only good to come from this crisis is an unprecedented opportunity to buy the assets of these institutions at auctions. When people think of the RTC they only think of real estate being available. The fact is that RTC sells all types of things. All the assets of the bank that went under will be sold. This includes everything from the office furniture and fixtures to all the branches' buildings. In addition to the assets of the bank, all of the bad loans and the corresponding properties they represent will be sold as well.

I had recently attended an RTC auction of a bank branch. All the office equipment was advertised to be sold along with office furniture and "assorted items". When I inspected the assets I was very surprised to find what I did. On the top floor of the bank I found living quarters for some person connected with the bank to use. There was a complete king size bedroom set, a complete living room set and a complete gym. Even with my experience, I was surprised to see this. The quality of these items were top grade, and they looked brand new. I was not prepared to buy any furniture that day, especially since my wife has the final say about furniture, but I did buy some gym equipment and got a great deal. I bought a professional "Liferower" video type rowing machine, that you commonly see in health spas, for $100.00. When I had it delivered I called the manufacturer to get an instruction book and gave them the serial number of the machine. It turned out that this machine was their top of the line machine and was delivered to the bank four months earlier at a cost of $3,467.00 and I bought it for $100!!! Now the machine has a place of honor in the gym I had built in my home and collects dust just as well as all the other equipment I had purchased at other auctions. The moral to this story is that RTC will sell the assets that were accumulated by these easy spending bank executives, and some of them have purchased some extravagant items. You can find just about anything at some of these auctions, from fine art to gym equipment.

The RTC is an organization whose form is changing very frequently. They had opened many district offices and have just consolidated many of those same offices. You can get a complete list of the RTC offices that now exist in Part 7 of this book. Due to the changing nature of RTC, I would suggest that when you contact the appropriate office, you should inquire if any new offices may be responsible for an area that is of interest to you.

The RTC is one of the best sources for real estate of all federal agencies. Their inventory contains everything from brand new skyscraper office buildings to single and multi-family homes and even raw land. There are a few ways that you can deal with the RTC when purchasing property. First thing you must do is to obtain a list of the properties. You may have some difficulty in obtaining this, but keep after it until you come across someone who knows what they are doing.

I would suggest you get a listing of all of the RTC offices for the following reason. The assets of a bank are disposed of by the district office located nearest the bank's main office. Many of these banks have bad loan assets all over the country. So a bank in Denver that has been taken over by the Denver RTC office may have an apartment building in New York. If you wanted to buy this asset you must contact the Denver office. In fact, they could conduct an auction in Denver for an asset in New York and local New Yorkers may be in the dark about it.

You can purchase property from RTC in two different ways. First, they list the properties with Realtors. The prices they ask for are the appraised values they have established for the property. Sometimes these appraised values are at good levels and sometimes they are far too high. Nevertheless, RTC will use the appraisal as a basis for them to negotiate from. As a rule of thumb, the RTC can accept an offer equaling 80% of the appraised value. Some sources state that they can accept a 70% offer without special consideration. If you see a piece you like, put in a discounted offer and see what happens.

If the property is appraised at a level that is over priced, put in an offer that you think is fair. If RTC just receives offers of this type they will eventually order a new appraisal and will use that as their basis to negotiate from. Your dealings with RTC on an offer type transaction will be largely influenced by who in RTC is handling the asset. If you get a hard nosed type then he may not feel like taking your offer even if it falls in accepted parameters. Yes, personalities do come into play here. They can site some internal regulation and not accept your offer and hold out for a better one. Sometimes they may just decide to place the asset in the auction process which may net them a lower value than if they took your offer.

The other method of sale the RTC uses is the auction. Here you do not have to put up with anyone's ego. Usually a large number of properties are grouped for individual sale at an auction. You will see each property listed and assigned a lot number for sale. Along with a description of the property you will also see their appraised value and the date of the appraisal. As mentioned earlier, do not pay attention to these appraisals. Rely on your research, not theirs.

At the auction the property will be sold either absolute, regardless of price, or with a reserve where a certain price must be achieved, or with a "judgment reserve" where an official of RTC will decide, either on the spot or within a certain time period, to accept the highest bid. Since the RTC is charged with the liquidation of these assets at market levels, they are inclined to let the auction and their past marketing efforts establish the market and accept most of the bids received at an auction. They realize that an offer received prior to the auction will probably not be available now, since anyone who was interested enough to make an offer in the first place will probably attend the auction and witness the price reached with all of his competition in the same room.

The type of auctions the RTC uses are open verbal auctions conducted by private auctioneers. They may impose a financial restriction on attendance. This is commonly done to insure that only serious people are in the audience. To meet this restriction you must show the person at the registration table a check equal to a predetermined percent of a required deposit if you are the winning bidder. I have seen financial restrictions range from $1,000 to $50,000. The financial restriction should not bother you, since you would have to come up with at least that amount of money anyway at knockdown. It

THE WORLD OF AUCTIONS

is designed to keep the merely curious out. Otherwise their auctions are open to the public.

The inspection of the assets will vary with the asset type being sold. With property, the RTC will normally set up a couple of inspection dates for viewing the property. You may encounter some difficulty at these inspection dates. Based on my own personal experience they had an inspection date set on an occupied home. I went there only to find the tenant refusing access. Another time they had put a sign on a vacant piece of property identifying it as the parcel for sale; in fact the actual parcel was down the block. I suggest that if you find a parcel that is of interest to you, double check its location with the town tax maps.

With general merchandise, office equipment, furniture and fixtures the inspection of the assets is normally on the day of sale. You will probably have a few hours to take a look at what is being offered. This is important to attend the inspection period and not just arrive in time for the sale. Many times at RTC auctions you will find many items during the inspection period that were not advertised, thereby increasing your chances of getting a good deal.

The RTC will guarantee the buyer free and clear title. As always, I suggest the use of an attorney for any real estate transaction. They also will guarantee payment of a broker's commission of 2% on the sale of property if a broker brought you to the sale. If you are going to buy something, bring along a friend who happens to be a broker and enjoy the 2% payment you will receive. Watch out for the broker who attempts to get you to sign a brokers agreement at the inspection site. They are just trying to make money on the possibility you buy the property. You DO NOT have to sign any broker agreements for any of these RTC properties. I have heard cases where a broker has set up an official looking table and chairs during the inspection portion of the auctions and had everyone sign a broker agreement. I don't know if his scam was successful for him, but he sure tried hard. Remember, your signing any type of document is not a requirement to inspect these properties.

RTC has a generous budget for the auctioneers to spend on advertising. The sales are normally well advertised, although you may want more time to investigate a property than just from the advertisement date. Most auctioneers that deal with RTC maintain mailing lists, so get yourself on them. The RTC itself has a mailing program and you can get yourself on it by contacting an RTC office.

If you are in the market for a home for yourself, the RTC is the place to be. They have everything from condos to million dollar mansions. You can even get financing now on some property. In an attempt to increase the dollar value of some properties they offer very competitive rates to buyers with NO points. TAKE ADVANTAGE OF THIS. Just the time and headaches you will save by not dealing with a pain in the neck mortgage company will be worth it. It will also speed up and simplify your closing if the RTC gives you the loan. The down payment requirements are as low as 10% and for a first time home buyer using their financing is the best thing you can do! So many people stay away from the housing market because they cannot accumulate the 20-25% deposits or qualify for a mortgage. This is an answer to their prayers.

The results of auctions for properties that have been held by the RTC have been predictable. Most of the properties sold at a level equal to 60% of the appraised value that RTC provided. Almost every property sold. The RTC apparently examined all the associated costs of not selling the property and decided to liquidate it. This attitude of "getting it over with" is just what the auction buyer wants. A seller that is willing to part with the assets on the block regardless of the price is a wonderful thing. This means that you have the opportunity to get a great deal.

PART 2

CHAPTER 4

The General Services Administration (G.S.A.)

The General Services Administration's (G.S.A.) main function is to liquidate government surplus to the exclusion of the Department of Defense. The government surplus that is sold is new as well as used. Most of the assets once used by any government agency are sold by G.S.A., and they sell anything you can think of. G.S.A. is one of the largest sources for auctioned assets. Assets like desks, typewriters, cars, boats, planes, cameras, household items and much, much more are sold. Since the assets are surplus, most are in fair to poor condition. Many assets are damaged and may be able to be repaired. Others are severely damaged and may only be good for parts. Then there are the assets that are in perfect condition. These are what I suggest my readers to go after. The other assets may be of some interest to some, but I feel your time can be better spent at auctions with new assets.

G.S.A. uses in-house auctioneers employed by G.S.A. The main reason the government contracts with private contractors is because they find private firms can handle specific jobs more effectively, and usually less expensively, than the government. G.S.A. does not abide by this logic.

The sealed bid is used widely by G.S.A. because many assets are sold in bulk and are spread over large geographical areas. Due to the large distances where the assets are stored, physical inspection can be difficult and costly. Since most assets that are similar are in similar condition, many people only inspect the assets at the location that has the greatest amounts. They then gamble that the rest of the assets are in similar condition and bid accordingly. I do not like bidding on anything that is be sold "as is, where is" without inspecting it. Since most feel as I do, these assets generally sell for bargain prices. These sealed bid sales usually require a 20% deposit enclosed with your bid offer. If you are not the successful bidder your deposit will be refunded. If you are the successful bidder you will be contacted and told when you may make final payment and take possession.

Public auction: Auctions are held regularly at sights throughout the U.S. To find the location nearest you call 1-800-848-8924. These auctions are conducted like any other open verbal auction. The public auctions also usually require a 20% deposit in cash or certified funds. They are open to the general public and you must be at least 18 years old to bid.

Title: All assets with titles are sold free and clear of all and any liens. As in the U.S. Marshal sales you will receive a Federal title that can be exchanged for a state title in the state in which you live.

Real estate is also sold, but is very rare. You can call 1-800-472-1313 and be placed on a mailing list. This number is automated and gives you several choices for information to choose from. You can also write to U.S. Property Sales List Information Center, Pueblo, Colorado 81002. They will send you a list that comes out quarterly.

PART 2

CHAPTER 5

THE DEPARTMENT OF DEFENSE

The Department of Defense (DOD) routinely sells assets that they categorize as surplus. Just as GSA handles surplus assets for many other government agencies, the DOD will liquidate anything in their inventory that is surplus. I want you to just consider the size of the DOD and realize the great variety of items they have. It is not only guns and used jeeps, but everything that is needed to make the DOD function. That means everything from answering machines to X-ray machines and everything in between. With the Gulf War over and the Cold War won, the Defense Department is being scaled back. With all the troop reductions and the closing of many bases, the entire organization that supported them is now surplus and will be sold off.

The DOD is a great source for just about anything. The prices that people have paid for assets are legendary. No matter what business you are in, you will find something of interest for you at the DOD. Many people use the DOD as a source of income through the resale of assets they purchase from DOD. The DOD has stuff they don't even know they have. Their inventory control system needs a little work. Do not worry, you have not missed the boat. There are plenty of assets yet to be sold.

The DOD liquidates its assets with two methods. The first is the National Bidders List which sells large quantities, items in bulk and larger equipment through a sealed bid format. You can be included on the bidding list by writing or calling them at the numbers provided in part 7 of this book. You will receive an application that will give you some selections to make, such as geographic preference and type of merchandise you are interested in. Try to be as specific as possible with your selection. If you ask to receive everything you will drown in the amount of offerings you receive and spend all your time looking through them. Once you are on their sealed bid list you are expected to place a bid on a regular basis or you will be dropped from the list and will have to apply again. To maintain your mailings just submit a very low bid on something that may be of use to you if you buy it.

These sealed bid auctions provide the entrepreneur with the opportunity to make a lot of money if you get in the right situation. The stories I have heard attest to the ingenuity of some people. I know of a case where a man bought 25 WWII bombers for a couple of thousand dollars and had them cut up for scrap metal and made a nice big profit. You can find many ways to turn assets around for profit. You just have to use your head and your ingenuity.

The second method of liquidation that the DOD uses is localized offices, referred to as Defense Reutilization Marketing Offices (DRMO). These DRMO offices hold public open verbal auctions at various sites for the same surplus goods of the DOD. They lot the items in smaller quantities than the National Bidders List. You will not be faced with buying 100 desks at a time. With DRMO you can get one.

The DRMO will usually sell assets with an open verbal auction, but they also sell items at a set price, just like a store. The prices you will find on items sold this way will be about wholesale or better. The one big advantage to purchasing assets this way is the savings in time. If you see something you want, you just buy it. During the auction there may be so many lots before the one you are interested in, it could take hours. Your wait will normally be rewarded with money saved on the purchase of the item.

The terms and conditions of these auctions will vary from office to office. Generally, you will be able to put down a deposit and pay the balance in a few days. Make sure you understand all the terms and conditions. Even if you have attended several auctions at the same office, they can change the terms at any time.

You can get a complete listing of all the DRMO offices in Part 7 of this book. Contact them by phone or by mail and attend a few of them to see if they of interest to you.

PART 2

CHAPTER 6

The Internal Revenue Service

The Internal Revenue Service (IRS), as we all know, is the Federal Tax collector. They are empowered to collect taxes and seize assets for non-payment. The IRS can and will seize anything a person owns of value for failing to pay their taxes. Houses, jewelry, cars, boats, planes and businesses are just some of the assets that can be seized. To add to their power, fines and imprisonment can go along with their seizures for the tax offenders. I believe it was Mr. Perot who said in a speech something like, "To pay taxes is an honor. If you're paying a lot of taxes you're making a lot of money." Many people do not believe that statement, and they are the ones who enable us to buy at IRS sales.

When a home is seized for non-payment of taxes the defendant is given a certain amount of time to repay their taxes with interest and penalties. If the tax judgment is large, the property may be sold. Because the IRS is protecting the loyal tax payers, in an effect to recoup the lost tax dollars they have an interesting method of sale. Most of the IRS sales are sealed bids, but they may conduct an open verbal auction. If you are the highest bidder you will not receive a deed to the property. Instead you will have to wait 180 days, the tax offender's time limit to pay their taxes, penalty and interest. In that time you will receive a high interest rate of 20% on your money. This interest is added to the tax offender's debt. If they do not pay their taxes, penalty and interest after the 180 days you will be given the property's title.

Now, before you run to buy something from the IRS you should know that the property is NOT sold free and clear of liens. It is very possible you could investigate the property and think there are no liens only to have some large undetected lien appear, ruining your deal. If this happens you quite possibly would have been better off buying a similar property at a retail price. I hate to buy retail! Most of the time, if a property is investigated for liens the odds are in your favor that no undetected lien will appear. This makes an IRS real estate sale a fairly good gamble. If everything goes the way it should you will either be repaid plus get the high interest on your money or become the owner of the property.

Do not make the mistake some people do and buy an IRS house because you feel there is no way the tax offender will let their house be lost and you can make all that interest. Remember to set your price as if you were going to take possession because you may just have to.

If the IRS chooses, they will let the U.S. Marshal sell anything else they may have.

To contact the IRS simply call the office nearest you or the office nearest the areas you are interested in and ask for the telephone number for IRS asset liquidations. Most cities have a recorded message briefly describing the property and the time, date and place of the sale. Always call the day before the sale to make sure the sale is still on.

PART 2

CHAPTER 7

THE UNITED STATES POSTAL SERVICE

The United States Postal Service (USPS) has a varied policy toward the auctioning of various assets. The USPS acquires assets for sale in three different ways. First, anything that gets lost or is not able to be delivered will be auctioned off. Second, the surplus assets of the USPS, such as trucks and equipment, may be sold by them at auction. Third, the USPS has the ability to seize assets as a result of postal fraud, and these may be auctioned also. I will discuss these in more detail below.

The sale of undeliverable or unclaimed merchandise is held on a regular basis at one of five regional sale facilities. These facilities are in New York City, San Francisco, Philadelphia, Atlanta and St. Paul. If you are near one of these facilities and want to have some fun, I would attend one of these sales. You can find just about anything that can be mailed at these auctions. You will be able to inspect the items before the sale and the terms are usually cash and carry. The prices at these auctions are normally very cheap, so prepare to get a bargain.

The USPS will sell its surplus vehicles and equipment by either auctioning it off themselves or by turning the assets over to GSA (read more about GSA in Chapter 4) for liquidation. The USPS has several locations at which they auction their vehicles. These locations are listed in Part 7 of this book. You can also just simply call your post office and ask them where the closest sale location is.

The sale of seized and confiscated goods can be accomplished at the discretion of the Postal Inspector In Charge of a particular case. The Postal Inspectors confiscate all types of assets for individuals guilty of mail fraud and other offenses. They commonly seize cars, boats and other assets, just as DEA or the United States Marshal would. Once the property has been forfeited to the United States, the Inspector will determine how to liquidate them. Sometimes they will turn the assets over to GSA or to the U.S. Marshal for liquidation. We commonly sell cars at our auctions for the postal service.

To find out what will be sold from the Inspectors may be difficult, since they commonly turn the assets over to other agencies for liquidation. Occasionally the USPS will sell these items themselves or through an auctioneer they hire. In these circumstances you will have the opportunity to catch the advertisements for these sales. If you see an advertisement for a sale of this type, I would suggest attending it because they are usually not well attended and you may get a good deal. These auctions are held infrequently and the terms and conditions will vary from all cash to a cash deposit with the balance due in a check. You will receive a free and clear title for any vehicles you may buy from the USPS.

PART 2

CHAPTER 8

OTHER AGENCIES WHICH MAY AUCTION ASSETS

THE FEDERAL DEPOSIT INSURANCE CORPORATION (FDIC) The FDIC is a great source through which to directly purchase a home. The properties are not auctioned off as yet, but they may be changing that policy soon. The FDIC is the agency that is responsible for the banks that are in the Federal Reserve System, just as the Resolution Trust Corporation is responsible for all the Savings and Loans. When a commercial bank becomes insolvent the FDIC will take control of the assets of the bank and dispose of them. With the potential of more commercial banks going under you will see more and more auctions from the FDIC.

The FDIC currently uses auctions to dispose of the business assets, like furniture, fixtures and equipment of the banks it has taken over. As their current methods of liquidation become overworked, they will look to the auction methods used by RTC to successfully liquidate property. You will find a listing of FDIC offices, which you should contact regarding the auctioning of assets that are of interest to you. This is a developing area for FDIC, so be patient with your inquiries and keep in contact with them. Do not rely on receiving information from them about future auction events. They currently do not have that capability. I suggest contacting them once per month so that you won't miss anything.

FEDERAL NATIONAL MORTGAGE ASSOCIATION (Fannie Mae) FEDERAL HOME LOAN MORTGAGE ASSOCIATION (Freddie Mac) Both of the above agencies play a major part in the financing of mortgages in the United States. They become the custodian of many houses as a result of default of the borrower on the loan. These homes have been traditionally marketed through brokers and directly by the agencies.

Recently these agencies have been liquidating properties through auctions. These agencies are finding that the fastest and most efficient way to sell large numbers of properties is through an auction. You will usually find a reserve placed on the sale lots to insure the agencies receive a certain dollar value. These reserve prices are a function of the outstanding loan on the property. If the market for the property has not crashed through the level of the loan value, then you may see a reserve price that is very reasonable.

The use of auctions as a method of liquidation for these agencies is relatively new. They are achieving good results with them, so I believe they will expand these programs. When you contact them ask to receive all the information they can provide you on their listings and the listings that are going for auction. It is important to get their general listings, as well, because the properties to be sold at auction will be compiled from existing inventories. You may find a house that you fall in love with in the general listings and can request information on the possibility of it going to auction.

THE SMALL BUSINESS ADMINISTRATION (SBA) The SBA is an agency that helps provide capital to small businesses through a program of grants or guarantees for loans issued by a bank to a qualified borrower. When you apply for an SBA guaranteed loan through a lending institution you will be required to pledge certain assets as security for the loan. The security requirements are varied as to the type of assets, so you may find equipment, real and personal property pledged against the loans.

If your loan defaults either the lending institution or SBA will foreclose on the pledged assets. If SBA gets control of the assets they will either auction them off or hit the ball back to the lender and let them dispose of the assets. SBA is not set up as a liquidator of large quantities of property, so they hire private auctioneers to handle the sale details. When they do sell assets at auction they are looking to recoup the loan value or something close to it. Most SBA loans have been paid down so the SBA may be only looking for 60% to 80% of the asset's value to satisfy the loan. As a result you may be able to pick up some good deals.

The Terms and Conditions at such auctions will change from sale to sale. Pay special attention to title transfers and guarantees. Another area of concern is the delivered status of real property; will it be delivered vacant? The payment terms can range from cash at knockdown to your purchase being subject to financing.

When you contact SBA, ask them if they have any assets that they will auction off and which auctioneers will do the sale. Contact all those auctioneers and request to be placed on their mailing lists for upcoming SBA and all other sales. The more mailings you receive the greater your prospects of getting something good.

Part Three

PART 3

CHAPTER 1

UNITED STATES BANKRUPTCY COURT (USBC)

The United States Bankruptcy Court is one of the most important sources of auctions for assets of all descriptions. The function of the court is to permit individuals and businesses to either reorganize their financial business affairs or oversee the orderly liquidation of assets to satisfy creditors.

When a company or an individual find themselves in the predicament of not being able to meet their obligations or debts, they can petition the United States Bankruptcy Court (USBC) for protection from their creditors. This is referred to as voluntary bankruptcy. Many times the creditors petition the court for protection of their interest from the continued actions of the debtor. This is called involuntary or forced bankruptcy. In either case the USBC will decide what will be done with the assets of the debtor.

Depending on which chapter of the bankruptcy code is used, the court will act accordingly. If Chapter 7 is used, this means the debtor has given up any chance to continue in business or admits he cannot pay all his bills now or in the future. In this case, the USBC will appoint a United States Trustee to handle the orderly disposition of the remaining assets and use the proceeds from such disposition to pay off the debtors with what is normally pennies on the dollar. When the USBC grants a Petition of Bankruptcy, the creditors will have no future claim on the debtor. The creditors will get their settlement and nothing else. Even if the debtor wins the lottery next week, once the proceedings have concluded, the creditors who may have received nothing will have no claim on future earnings.

If Chapter 11 is used, then the USBC will allow a reorganization. The petitioner will be protected by the USBC from actions of all the former creditors for a period of time. This will immediately put a stop to any foreclosure or repossession actions of the creditors. In order to give the company a chance to survive and likely give the existing creditors a greater chance to recoup their past debts, the petitioner will be able to do business with the protection of the USBC. Any new debts established while the company is under Chapter 11 protection will take priority over all other debts. This arrangement will give the company the ability to engage in business and possibly turn the company around.

All the plans the company makes during this period of Chapter 11 protection will need to be approved by the USBC. If the company gets its act together then the company may be able to emerge from Chapter 11 as a reorganized company. The company will come out of Chapter 11 with a settlement worked out with its previous creditors and the ability to continue in business in the future.

When a company or an individual goes into Chapter 11 bankruptcy protection, they may not be able to work out of their difficulties. In this event, the USBC will put the company into Chapter 7 proceedings and turn the assets over to a United States Trustee for liquidation of the assets. The Trustee will proceed with the orderly sale of the assets through various types of auctions, use the proceeds to pay off any new debts established under Chapter 11 and then pay the rest of the previous creditors.

Once the USBC hands the assets over to a Trustee, that is when it gets interesting to an auction buyer. The Trustee will hire a private auctioneer to sell the assets of the debtor. The function of the Trustee is to protect the interest of the creditors who will receive the proceeds of the sale minus the expenses of the sale. The Trustee is instructed by USBC to get "fair market value" for the assets. Since these assets are sold at auction you will find many of them auctioned subject to USBC approval.

The entire presumption of a bankruptcy proceeding is to bring an end to a bad situation. During the liquidation of assets I find that the USBC is not willing to hold out for a better price for extended periods of time for assets that are being sold. They are inclined to accept the "fair market value" of an item as being what it can fetch at an auction. They let the auction procedure establish the "fair market value" of an asset being sold under these circumstances. I find it very rare indeed, for an asset that has been sold subject to USBC approval not to get approved. If it does not get approved, the USBC will order it put up for sale again, and they will be more inclined to accept the value they receive as "fair market value".

What does this all mean to you? Well, the auction buyer can look at the Court's initials of USBC as meaning "United States Bargain Center". The USBC will sell assets of every possible description. When a company is liquidated, everything that company has is sold to satisfy the creditors. Just think for a moment what your company has and imagine it ALL being sold. Companies big and small will get sold off. Even huge companies get sold off. This means you will find anything and everything at USBC auctions.

During the Chapter 11 portion of bankruptcy you can even buy a division of a company or the entire company. It is common for a USBC judge to authorize the sale of a company as part of the restructuring plan. One such case was the Chapter 11 proceedings for the New York Daily News newspaper. The Judge wanted to sell the paper in an effort to save it and the corresponding jobs and creditors' interest. In this case, a type of auction was held by the Judge that was entertaining bids for the entire company. This was extremely complex and the bidders were able to make significant demands of the terms and conditions of the sale. The bidders did not simply say they would pay X millions for the company. They insisted on negotiating employment and union contracts that covered all aspects of the business and its ability to operate in the future. The bidders took a management view point in labor negotiations but they had a much, much stronger position, because if their conditions were not met there would be no sale and, therefore, no jobs. So the bidders were not only presented with an opportunity to purchase an asset, they were able to affect the condition of that asset. In these types of negotiations the bidder has the upper hand. The Judge wants to arrive at an acceptable conclusion but will put definite time constraints on all the parties involved. In these cases the creditors, the employees and the Court would like to see the company survive and the USBC sometimes puts great effort into achieving that outcome.

If you are looking into starting a new business, expanding your existing one or buying a different one, then you should definitely look into what the USBC has on their menu. There have been cases when a company was sold off to a bidder for nothing more than some guarantees by the new purchaser to support some of the old debt. The opportunities to purchase businesses, divisions or business assets are excellent. Many times, these assets and companies will cost you less than if you started them from scratch. These purchases can be complicated, so I recommend the use of a competent lawyer and accountant. With the large number of bankruptcies as a result of the fallout from the merger and acquisition binge of the 1980s you will see all types of businesses, from airlines to manufacturing facilities, come through the USBC. In these cases the bidder is definitely in a Buyers Market. Just look at some of the high profile cases in your area and you will see some outstanding values.

I attended a USBC bankruptcy auction of a building supply house and bought building materials at fantastic prices. Since my brother was building a house, I called him and asked him what he needed. He said everything, and lots of it! They had a huge selection of construction lumber and I was able to buy all the lumber he needed to build his house. For instance: he needed 2 X 10 lumber in 22 and 24 foot lengths for his floors and roof framing. The best price he was seeing in New York was about $21 each. I bought him 600 pieces for $1.10 each; a savings of $11,940.00. He also needed 2 X 4 lumber and 2 X 6 lumber in 10 and 16 foot lengths for his interior and exterior walls. I bought 1,200 of them for $.50 each when he was looking at a $12 average price; a savings of $13,800.00 My brother was one of the happiest guys on earth when I told him what I had bought. He had to spend $1,200.00 for a couple of tractor trailers to haul the lumber to his site and for a crane to hoist the lumber off the trucks. Even with that expenditure he did pretty well.

Whenever you hear of a USBC auction, GO TO IT! The prices I was able to get were far below the market for lumber at a lumber yard, but the court accepted them as "fair market value" because the entire supply yard was sold in one day with no delivery services and the building products market was in a slump at the time. In addition, as with most auctions, many people had no idea that an auction was even being held. I mentioned my purchase to a fellow that owned a lumber yard in Golden Bridge, N.Y. and he told me that if he had known about it he would have bought everything. At the prices lumber was selling for he said he would have made more money on the inventory that was being auctioned off than he had made all year. This illustrates my point that "Knowledge Equals Power and Money"

As mentioned earlier beware of look alike auctions. Everyone knows that Bankruptcy auctions are popular and many auctions try to pass themselves off as Bankruptcy. If you see an ad that is "By Order of Creditors" or "To Prevent Bankruptcy" realize that these auctions are not taking place at the order of a Federal Judge or United States Trustee. Do not be taken in by these ploys because if the sponsors of these auction are unscrupulous enough to try to misrepresent the reason for an auction who knows what other deceptions they are capable of.

To keep yourself informed of USBC auctions will require you to follow these instructions. You must make contact with the United States Trustees that are appointed by the USBC to handle the disposition of the assets. There are 21 districts, which are listed in Part 8 of this book, of United States Trustees. A

Trustee is appointed by the Court to handle the auction. The Trustee will hire an auctioneer to conduct the sale. Any Trustee can use as many different auctioneers as he chooses, so it is a little difficult to keep track of. To contact these Trustees call, write or visit the Trustee main office and ask them to provide you with a list of all the Trustees in that district. Whatever they require you to do to receive a list, follow their instructions. You may be required to provide them with a self-addressed envelope, or even visit them in person.

Once you have your list of Trustees contact them in writing or call and request all information regarding their procedures in liquidating the assets as ordered by the Court. Request a list of the auctioneers they commonly use and then contact the auctioneers and request to be placed on their mailing lists. Initially, this requires a bit of leg work, but it will be worth it when you start receiving notifications of upcoming sales. Also ask the Trustee if they require advertising of upcoming sales in a specific newspaper by the auctioneers they hire. As mentioned earlier it is important to get in the habit of looking through the auction advertising sections of your newspaper on a daily basis. You know that the day you do not look at the paper is the day the most fantastic auction will be advertised. So look every day. It only takes a few minutes but it could save you thousands.

The USBC normally holds open verbal auctions that are open to the public. Many times, financial restrictions are placed on an auction to assure that any people who attend are serious bidders. Most commonly, they require you to have a certified check with you for a specific amount to be admitted. With the sale of a company or a division of a company the Judge will normally expect you to demonstrate your ability to conclude your purchase.

The terms and conditions you will encounter are at the discretion of the United States Trustee who is handling a particular case. I have seen them range from all cash at knockdown to where a small deposit is required and the balance is due in a few days. Make sure you pick up your purchase as soon as possible to avoid problems of merchandise or component parts disappearing or becoming damaged. Always hold on to the receipts you receive at the auction to help you establish your claim should a problem develop.

Part Four

PART 4

CHAPTER 1

Real Estate Tax Sales

Real estate tax sales take place when someone does not pay their property taxes. As someone once said, "If you think you own your house and land try not paying your property tax and see who really owns it." Because many people find out the hard way, real estate tax sales are one of the best sources for purchasing real estate.

At real estate tax sales you should be able to get the best deals of all and have the highest potential profits or equity. In order to maximize your profits or equity you must first target an area and get thoroughly acquainted with the geographical differences of that area. You must also have a good understanding of what prices are in the current market. Prices in the same area sometimes vary dramatically, depending on many different factors. You must find these facts out before you attend the auction and set your predetermined maximum bid. Some things to investigate are the school district, taxes and the legal mailing name of the township the property you intend to buy belongs to.

Real estate tax sales are held by all local governments. They are usually advertised, but some townships only use the local public listings bulletin board at the County Clerk's office to serve as notice of the sale. Other larger municipalities, like New York City, have regularly scheduled auctions and maintain a mailing list, usually for a normal fee. Please note, New York City and other major cities may temporarily stop this type of program due to budget cuts. Contact your local County Clerk or call the Real Property Department or the Real Estate Tax Department to get this information.

At a real estate tax sale you will find all types of real estate, from commercial building to luxury single family homes. You can also find vacant land of all types and sizes. If someone does not pay their real estate taxes they will eventually forfeit their property and lose all interest to that property. You should note that most of the properties are located in lower income areas, but there are ample higher priced properties to keep anyone busy.

When you purchase a real estate tax property, some properties are sold free and clear of all liens and back taxes, but some properties are sold free of back taxes ONLY. The best tax sale properties are those sold totally free and clear. When you purchase these types of properties the Tax Department is responsible for any liens or back taxes. When purchasing tax sale properties that are not free and clear of liens and only free of back taxes, the purchaser is buying the property subject to any liens. Some cities and states, after a tax sale, allow a certain amount of time for the former owner to pay you back plus high interest and reclaim the property.

This system works much like the IRS sales. The successful bidder will receive interest on their money until the allowed time is expired. At that time, if the former owner does not pay you back in full, with interest, you will be given the property with all liens. Be sure to check with the agency conducting the sale on this matter. This matter of liens makes a world of difference on how much you should pay for a property. You will usually need a 20 or 25 percent deposit of the selling price at knockdown. The properties are sold without any contingency for financing so if you do not have the money, do not buy. You can and will lose your deposit if you cannot close.

The property is sold "as is, where is" and may have some contingency that runs with the land. A "right of way easement", "special uses requirement", or "structure restriction" are some of the most common contingencies. Do not buy a property thinking you can get the government to change its contingencies, because you most likely can not. Even if you can get them to change their requirements, it will take more time and money than you would expect.

Some local governments, as in New York City, in order to help liquidate tax sale property that they have taken ownership of and to get the highest price possible, will offer mortgages. Please note these mortgages are usually offered to qualified buyers only. If you do not qualify you still will be required to close in the contracted time or forfeit your deposit. The mortgage rates are usually competitive with other non-governmental rates and in some cases may be lower.

I have purchased a great deal of real estate through tax sales, and the well never seems to run dry. At a recent tax sale I purchased two homes in Suffolk County, New York. They were in need of repair, but after the repairs were complete they were both sold, and sold to the first persons who looked at each house. I know someone who bought a vacant piece of land for $35,000.00. After getting building permits at a cost of about $5,000.00 the property was sold to a builder for $350,000.00 one year later. You should know they had a government mortgage on the property and only invested $12,000.00 total out of pocket, to make $310,000.00 PROFIT. Were they lucky? Yes, but most of the time luck does not just happen. It is made. There is no reason why you, too, cannot make a good profit from real estate tax sales.

To find out about these sales contact any County Clerk or Department of Real Estate in the areas you are interested in. As mentioned earlier many larger municipalities have a mailing list you can be placed on for a normal fee. If there is no mailing list call the County Clerk. Some County Clerks will tell you there are too many different properties to tell you about and explain that they are listed on the County Clerks bulletin board. These lists have a habit of disappearing. You should always call the County Clerks office to be sure there is some property listed for sale before you check their bulletin board. If there is a list posted ask someone in the Clerks office if the list is complete and if any properties have been added or taken off.

PART 4

CHAPTER 2

State and Local Surplus Sales

In every state, city, town, and village throughout America surplus properties and assets are sold off or destroyed when the item is replaced or is no longer needed. These assets are liquidated in much of the same manner in which the Federal sales are conducted. Since the municipalities do not liquidate assets on a regular basis a private auction firm is usually called in.

At these sales you can find assets ranging from typewriters and police cars to heavy equipment and land. Each municipality may have different methods of informing the public, but the odds are you will find the sales information somewhere in the town hall or at the County Clerks office. Larger cities may contract with an auction company to handle these sales. To find these sales call the County Clerk in the area you are interested in.

I know a man who bought a never used sit down lawn mower for only $100.00. This mini tractor retails for well over $1,000.00, but because the township he bought it from, decided they did not need it he was able to get a great deal at auction. Once you start attending auctions you will see stories like these in our book happen right before your eyes. Hopefully some of the great success stories will be yours.

PART 4

CHAPTER 3

City Marshal Sales

The City Marshals normally do not have auctions. On occasion, the City Marshals may have an auction and the asset may be of any type. You should know the City Marshals are in business for themselves. They are appointed by the Mayor and charge the public a fee to serve warrants issued from civil court and small claims court. It was reported that one of the New York City Marshals was the highest paid official in the city, earning over $500,000.00.

The City Marshals' main business is to serve eviction notices for landlords. If someone does not comply with a civil court or small claims court order, the City Marshal may seize assets to pay for the court ordered judgment. Anything owned may be seized, including bank accounts. If personal property is seized it is this property that may be auctioned. There are, however, certain properties that are exceptions and cannot be seized. These properties differ from city to city.

The City Marshals also are in the business of towing and selling at auction some of the scofflaw cars. At their sales the cars are NOT sold free and clear. Also note, most of the cars they handle are in poor condition.

In the last ten years of carefully following all types of auctions I have never purchased anything from a City Marshal sale. I can only remember coming across a very few sales in that time, and the assets were not of any interest to me.

If you are interested in City Marshal sales you are going to have to call the City Marshals in the area you are interested in. I suggest you spend your time on investigating other auctions described in this book.

PART 4

CHAPTER 4

Sheriff Sales

Sheriffs in large metropolitan cities with police departments are mainly empowered as the main collection agency for the city. Unlike Andy of Mayberry they do not protect the citizens and arrest the town drunk. They can make arrests but rarely do. Instead, they work much like the City Marshal and are sometimes in direct competition. One main difference is the Sheriffs are civil servants and not a private business like the City Marshals are. Another difference is that they can collect on judgments from the State Supreme Court. In a city like New York, with many people not paying their parking summons, it is the Sheriff who goes out and seizes cars and trucks for non-payment. Besides paying for towing and legal fees, the car or truck owner must pay the summons or tickets with penalties or have their property auctioned off. Because many of the vehicles get ticket after ticket, it often does not pay for the owner to pay the summons owed. You can often get a very nice deal at a Sheriff's auction. You should note, more times than not the vehicles are in poor condition and may need extensive repairs, so temper your bids accordingly.

If you are interested in a fine exotic car, the Sheriff's auction in New York is not for you. You might do much better in Miami, Los Angeles, and especially Broward County, Florida, but you will certainly find what you want at a U.S. Marshal or Customs auction.

To find out about what the Sheriff is selling off contact the Sheriff's Department in the area you are interested in. The Sheriff Departments in all the main cities do not maintain a mailing list, so you are going to have to call them periodically.

PART 4

CHAPTER 5

Police Sales

The police departments across America collect all types of assets and periodically sell them of at auction. Some of the most common assets are household items, baby strollers, bikes, radios, cars and trucks. When attending a police sale remember, most sales of cars and trucks are sold without ever starting the vehicle, so be sure to bid accordingly. Before you attend a police sale you should know most of their assets are in poor condition and are normally not worth your time. You should note because of the general poor condition few people attend and prices are usually very low. From time to time an asset in very good condition is sold and that is when the best deal occurs, but unless you go prepared to buy you may miss out. As the saying goes, "You've got to be in it to win it." Most police auctions will supply you with a list of the assets being offered for auction, but, unfortunately, they will make you go to the inspection sight to get the list. The inspection is usually the day of the sale but some police departments have inspection the day before the sale. If the sale is the same day as the inspection I suggest you pass by to see if anything of interest is being offered. If you are going, go with enough deposit money (usually 20%) in case you decide to stay.

Some police departments may require you to pay for and remove all properties upon final knockdown. Luckily, most police sales that require this have inspection the day before the sale or will have inspection early enough on the day of the sale to allow you to get to your bank. Many people ask me if they want to spend $7,000.00 on a car, if the car sells for less how do they bring the proper funds if they do not want to bring a lot of cash. My answer is bring several certified checks and some cash. If I were going to spend $7,000.00 for a certain asset I would bring two checks, one for $4,000.00 and one for

THE WORLD OF AUCTIONS

$2,000.00, and I would take $1,000.00 in cash. If, for some reason, the car sells for $3,500.00, you simply overpay and the auctioneer will refund the difference once your check has cleared. To avoid any possible problems I suggest not overpaying at any auction other than a government sale.

I know someone who is in the car service (taxi) business. He buys a large percentage of the cars used in his fleet at police auctions. Because most cars are in poor condition he pays very low prices and fixes them up. When your operating costs are reduced that is always good business. Another person I know is in the auto salvage business. He buys all the cars no one else wants for practically nothing and sells the car parts for a very big profit. Still another man bought his entire family's bikes in perfect condition and paid pennies on the dollar.

To find out about Police Sales contact police headquarters in the area you are interested in.

PART 4

CHAPTER 6

Surplus City and State Owned Real Estate

The Department of Transportation (D.O.T.) or comparable branch of government in most cities and states will sell of surplus real estate. This real estate can be some of the best values for the buyer because so few people attend their sales. Few people attend these sale because they are not usually well advertised.

I have seen farms located next to main highways sell for far less than market value. Many of the Department of Transportation's properties are zoned for commercial use, commercial meaning you cannot build single family homes on the property.

This type of property may sell for pennies on the dollar, but is usually still more than the average person can afford because most of the properties offered are very large. That fact is another reason why so few attend, and prices are low.

If the Department of Transportation had planned a road or the continuation or expansion of an existing road, they probably had control over the land for that road for years. When the government finally decides not to built, expand or extend the road, that land becomes surplus and will be sold off. You probably have some road or highway in your area that just ends. The vacant property around the incomplete road may be owned by the D.O.T. and eventually will be sold off.

Sometimes a smaller piece of property becomes available for sale and that is when you can get a really great deal. To find out about these sales contact the Department of Transportation in the area you are interested in.

City and State Department of Real Estate: Here is where you can find the best deals of all. Surplus real estate and real estate that has been taken over by the City or State for a number of reasons will be sold, usually semi-annually. Cities like New York have auctions every two to three months, according to the supply. As mentioned earlier, many times, to allow the buyer to buy a property he normally could not afford and at the same time let the city or state get the highest price possible, a mortgage is offered. Remember, although the qualifications are relaxed the successful bidder must qualify for the mortgage or risk losing their deposit.

At these sales you can find any type of real estate, from vacant land or single family homes to large buildings. In the last few years some of the properties offered have been sold with a restriction for owner occupied. This simply means you cannot sell the property for a number of years. As you can imagine, these properties sell for the lowest prices.

Some properties sell with a zoning restriction. This means you are only allowed to build what the zoning calls for. If the zoning calls for single family houses on 10,000 square feet of land you cannot build anything but a single family home. Before you buy any city or state real estate make sure you understand the zoning requirements.

Many of the properties that are taken over by the city or state are abandoned and need extensive repair. Fortunately, in most cities or states, low interest funding is available. In some cases you can get government grants to assist in the renovations. Many times, even though you have a 75% or 80% mortgage on the property you can still get government grants. This is especially true with low income or homeless projects.

I buy city and state real estate more than any other type of property. I am happy to say that in all my years of purchasing this type of property I have never had a bad experience. When buying from the city or state I even do without an attorney because the real estate is sold free and clear of all liens and taxes. If you are unfamiliar with the purchasing process it may be in your best interest to get an attorney.

The person who bought the property for $35,000 and later sold it for $350,000, bought it from this type of auction. I know someone who bought prime ocean front land in Staten Island, New York, for $80,000. This property was large enough for five houses. If you know anything about ocean front property in New York, then you know that $80,000 is pennies on the dollar. Another man bought a whole vacant block for the price of a single lot. Still another man bought a house in Florida for half its retail price. The success stories go on and on. With a little bit of money and knowledge you, too, can get a great deal.

Someone once asked me why does the city and state sell off property for less than it is worth. I answered, "It is easy to accept a lower than market price when the land did not cost them anything and the sale will also bring the city and state tax revenues." Also be advised that most of the parcels have minimum upset prices. If a property is passed because the minimum upset is too high the parcel will be sold at another time, usually with a much lower upset price. Normally, the city or state sets reasonable low minimum upset prices in order to attract bidders.

Most city and state real estate auctions have printed booklets describing the properties. Some booklets include a tax map and picture of some or all of the properties. These booklets are available for a nominal charge, and some cities offer them free. Some cities and states maintain a mailing list and most charge a fee. Be sure you are on any city or state mailing list you are interested in. To get this information contact the Department of Real Property and speak to someone in the sales division of the areas you are interested in.

Part Five

STATE AND LOCAL JUDICIAL SOURCES OF AUCTIONS

INTRODUCTION

The various courts that make up our state and local court systems handle many cases that will result in an auction being held to satisfy a judgment of the court. These courts rule on a wide variety of situations that require an order of the court to reach a solution. You will commonly see auctions held in cases of divorce, civil suits, foreclosures or trust deeds actions against property and probate decisions.

The resulting auctions will offer you an opportunity to purchase a wide variety of items at some very good prices. I have found that divorce cases, especially nasty ones, offer the best opportunity to get a deal. In these cases you may have two opposing sides that will do just about anything to hurt the other side, including hurting themselves by letting jointly owned real estate be sold at auction on the court house steps for a low price. Most often the parties will attempt to sell a jointly owned asset the conventional way, but if time is a factor they may choose an auction as a method of liquidation.

I know of a case where a good friend of mine bought a beautiful house on the south shore of Long Island, New York at an auction to remedy a divorce case. He bought a relatively new 3,800 square foot home for $167,000 when the market for a comparable home was $215,000. That was quite a savings, but the weird thing was that the people who had owned the house remarried and asked to buy the house back from my friend at a profit. He did not sell to them and still lives there today. I have no idea if the couple is still together. In these divorce cases, reason is sometimes put on the back burner to the benefit of the auction buyer.

PART 5

CHAPTER 1

REAL ESTATE FORECLOSURE AUCTIONS

The sale of real estate as a result of a foreclosure offers the auction buyer many opportunities to acquire property at some excellent levels. When an individual or company does not pay the note on property it has financed, the lender will go through a foreclosure proceeding to have the property sold and, hopefully, collect the amount that is owed to them. Some states have Trust Deeds instead of mortgages, and the procedures of foreclosure are different but the result is the same. You will be able to purchase the foreclosed property at an auction.

The fact that a property will be sold at auction does not automatically mean you will get a great deal. What commonly happens when a property is foreclosed on is that the lien holder will bid in their interest in the property. For example, if a bank was owed $200,000 on the property and it were to be placed on the auction block that bank could bid its $200,000 or any portion of that amount at the auction. The bank may do this to protect their interest, but many times they just prolong the inevitable. If they bid in their interest and no one else bids higher, then the bank will have bought the property. This may turn out to be either good or bad for the bank. If the "real world" value of the property is higher than their bid then they may resell the property for the loan amount or higher and get out of the property without a loss. If the property value is in actuality lower than their bid, then they are stuck with a property they will not be able to sell at the level they want. Holding and marketing the property will only add to the loss they may have to take to finally sell the property. The cost of taxes and maintenance will be the responsibility of the bank, so every day the bank does not sell the property the more it will cost them.

I see this trend more and more today in this falling real estate market. The bank, or more probably their lending officer, is reluctant to take the loss on the property by accepting whatever the bid price may be at the auction as the "market price". I hear statements from these people such as, "We're not going to give this property away" or "Our research values the property at a greater level than this auction would bring". Well, the surprise that awaits most of these people is that their unrealistic expectations of the market place will end up costing them more money down the road.

The motivation for this may be self preservation on the part of the loan officer or the branch manager of the bank. If the property is in their inventory then the loss does not hit the books yet, so they don't look bad. Some banks have decided to get on with business by taking their losses and not try to wait out a slow real estate market. Sooner or later these properties will be sold and many may be sold by the bank at auction.

At a foreclosure auction that does not have the lender bidding in its interest you normally have a better opportunity to get a good deal. These auctions will normally sell you a piece of property that will be guaranteed by the court to be free and clear of all liens. The Terms and Conditions will vary widely at these auctions. You may be required to pay all cash at the sale or have 30 to 60 days to close. Normally these auctions are not subject to you obtaining financing, so please pay special attention to all terms.

I have been observing a recent trend developing that is slightly reducing the amount of properties coming for sale. As a result of the many real estate courses and seminars that are popular today I have found that some of the properties are sold just prior to the auction date. These real estate courses teach you to track down a piece of property that is being auctioned and approach the current owner with a deal that will help them put some money in their pocket. With an auction, if the property sells for more than the loan value then the former owner will receive the balance of funds once the loans have been paid off. That is a big "IF" for the owner. He may not be looking at getting any money at all from the property. The deal that is offered to the owner, in effect, will buy his position for a lump sum of money. For example, if the property which is being foreclosed has an outstanding loan of $150,000 the student of these real estate courses may offer the owner $5,000 - 10,000 to take over his position. The overriding premise to this deal is that the property has a value that is higher than the outstanding loan and the lump sum payment. The owner is strongly motivated by the money being put on the table and may jump at the chance to put something in his pocket. This may be more appealing than to face the uncertainty of what, if anything, he will walk away with after his property is auctioned.

In light of this development I would still recommend waiting for the house to come to the auction block unless it is your dream house. If that is the case you may wish to insure your ability to own the house by approaching the owner and offering him a deal. You may not even have to offer any money if you can illustrate that your taking his position will preserve his credit rating or provide some other benefit. Most of the people who find themselves in these situations have done a pretty good job of ruining their credit rating already, so you may find the salvation of their credit worthiness a hard thing to sell.

You can keep track of what properties are going to be auctioned in a number of ways. The easiest way is to subscribe to a service that tracks foreclosures on a weekly basis. Many service firms have been established to provide this service. The cost of these services vary and the extent of the information they provide will vary as well. The subscriptions will range in price from $50 to $500 annually. This is a lot of money to spend, but it will save you the time and effort of doing the research yourself. These service companies normally advertise their services in the real estate sections of you local papers.

Another method of keeping track of auctions is to check with the court that has jurisdiction to view the posted notices. Most courts in the country will post notices of upcoming auctions in the building lobby or at the steps of the court. These notices are open to the public and you can view them during business hours. In addition, the court will require each auction to be advertised in a local newspaper. Contact the court and request a list of papers that are commonly used to advertise the sale.

When buying real estate at auction you may encounter some difficulty inspecting the house. In many instances the home will be occupied by the owner that is about to have his property sold by the court ordered foreclosure auction. Needless to say, individuals like this could not be called "happy campers," and to expect their cooperation in viewing their home may be optimistic. Realistically, you may have to make some value judgements about the condition of the house from the outside. This is obviously not the best way to do it, but it is better than nothing. At least you will see that it is still standing. If you like the outside of the house then go to the town building department with some notification of the court ordered sale and ask to see the plans of the house that are on file. They may give them to you if you explain the situation to them. This may help you get an idea of the inside structure of the house.

When determining your bid price limit in a situation where access is limited, I suggest you assume the worst. You must buy the house cheap enough to afford all the potential repairs that may be required. You may be faced with a situation where the kitchen and the bathrooms are in bad repair. All the plumbing may be bad and on and on. So when setting your limit anticipate these problems. If you don't find any problems then you made out well. Do not be afraid that you will under bid the house because all the other bidders will be in the same boat with limited ability to inspect the house. If the other bidders are prudent they will not move the price of the house to the level of one that they have had every opportunity to inspect.

If you are lucky enough to be the winning bidder on one of these foreclosed properties that may be occupied by the previous owner, you may have some difficulty in getting the property in a vacant condition. These same people who can make your inspection of the property all but impossible may have protection under the law from being removed from your house. Some localities offer a squatter all sorts of protection from being evicted. It seems incredible, but it is true. It could take you several months to get the old owners out of your new home. It is important to check with your attorney, local sheriff or marshal about eviction procedures. Also, make sure you ask the auctioneer or the sponsor of the auction if the house will be delivered vacant. Most of the time they will tell you that you are buying the house "AS IS". You may have some difficulty in getting the people out then figure that into your bid price limit. If the auctioneer or the sponsor agree to deliver the house in a vacant status make sure you have that condition in writing on your receipt or purchase contract. If the vacancy of the house becomes a problem then it is their problem, not yours. They will be responsible for all the costs until the house can be delivered vacant. Many auctions do guarantee a vacant house for the buyer, but many don't. Just be aware that this should be a consideration when looking at a piece of property.

If you are planning to buy a house, I strongly suggest that you look into foreclosure auctions. If you do not come across something you like then search the other sources of auctions such as RTC or U. S. Customs or the other sources we have discussed. The money you can save could be very significant. As I mentioned in the Forward of this book, you must look at how much money you would need to earn and then pay taxes on to get a true sense of the savings you will reap. Some people do not think the amount saved is worth all the trouble, but they are as wrong as can be. If you are a young couple just starting out, then a $10,000 savings will pay for a new child's college education if it is invested now. Anytime that you can purchase an asset that you want for less than the normal market price you are fulfilling your goals and fattening your bank account. Remember, money doesn't grow on trees! But if you're smart you can make money as easily as picking it off a tree!

I want to alert my readers of a popular scam regarding foreclosure auctions. You will encounter some look alike auctions for "Foreclosed" property. These are arranged to appear as a Court ordered sale of property when, in fact, the Court has nothing to do with the sale. Some banks or finance companies will advertise property that they foreclosed on, and had bid in their interest at the real court ordered auction to acquire the property, as being sold at an auction as foreclosed property. This property is no longer a foreclosure case because the Court is out of the picture.

The property is actually a REO (real estate owned by the bank) and should not be represented in its previous status. The motivation for doing this is to increase the attendance at an auction. More people are interested in court ordered auctions than what they really have, which is a private sector auction. You should also beware of Realtors using an auction to attempt to sell property for retail prices. There are no deals to be found there! Your attendance at real foreclosure auctions is a must. Sooner or later you will find that a great deal has landed in your lap. You must be prepared to take advantage of these auctions by having the proper funds available, and you must be able to meet all the terms and conditions. I know people who have built their entire fortune with the purchase of foreclosed properties. With the economic fallout of the 80's more and more properties have been foreclosed on, providing the auction buyer with plenty of opportunities to get a deal. I want my readers to participate in these savings.

PART 5

CHAPTER 2

OTHER COMMON CAUSES FOR COURT ORDERED AUCTIONS

The local court system handles a few other areas that significantly contribute to the number of auctions that are held. These are divorce cases, probate cases and judgment awards from civil cases. These areas, combined with the real estate foreclosure proceedings, account for a large percentage of all the auctions resulting from judicial intervention.

In the case of divorce, a judge will oversee the disbursement of assets between husband and wife. It does not always go smoothly in these cases, where the wife gets the house and the husband gets the car. Many times assets are directed to be turned into cash so that they may be easily divided. If the asset is a house, car, boat or business, etc., they can try to sell them the conventional method or they can turn to an auction. Considering that time is a factor in the settlement of many of these cases, an auction will expedite the liquidation of any asset.

The Terms and Conditions you will encounter at these auctions will vary. They are determined by the judge after considering motions by the attorneys in the case. In general, you will find they will want a quick closing, 30 days, for real estate transactions and cash at the sale for most other assets. Your inspection of these assets should be relatively easy, but you may encounter a disgruntled spouse making your life difficult. Once you have checked into the value of the asset I would strongly suggest looking into the eviction proceedings rule in your locality. You must prepare for all possible developments when you are dealing with real estate. Consult your attorney regarding the above.

Another good source of auctions arises from probate cases that settle the estates of the deceased. I have seen all types of assets at these auctions. Many times you will see auctions that are advertised as "Estate Auctions", but the Court is already out of the picture. These auctions may contain the assets that were left to the family of the deceased that the family will turn over to an auction house for liquidation. This is really a private sector auction because it is not directed by the court, but they have the potential of being some of the best auctions for you to attend. Just be careful that the auction appears to be genuine and not someone just selling off a bunch of junk.

Your inspection of assets at auctions held at these auction houses will normally be a few hours before the sale. The terms are normally cash at knockdown, but you will frequently encounter auctions where you can leave a deposit and pay your balance in a few days. When purchasing assets which have titles, such as cars and boats from an auction that is not court ordered, be careful as to who has the authority and ability to transfer title to you. I know of a case where a man purchased a car from the son of a man that had just died. As it turned out the purchaser had only given a deposit on the car and was about to pay for the rest when the family found out what was going on and stopped the sale. The son had no legal right to sell the car and the buyer would have had a problem if he had concluded the sale. All he had was some difficulty in eventually getting his deposit returned. So, in these cases, take some extra precautions regarding the sale of all assets.

Another area where the court gets involved is in a civil case. When you sue someone for damages you may receive a judgment to recover a dollar amount from the other party. This does not always mean that a check will be given to you by the other party. Many times your aggravation will just begin when you try to collect your money. What will normally happen is that your lawyer will hire a local marshal or sheriff that will attempt to collect the money owed in the judgment. They can levy your property and/or your wages. In some cases they may seize some assets and sell them off at an auction to raise money to satisfy the judgement.

If they are selling an asset they can only transfer the rights, title and interest in the asset to the buyer. This means that you will be buying an asset that may not be free and clear of all liens. The car or boat you buy may have a significant amount owed to someone that you will now be responsible for. The situation at these auctions is similar to what you will encounter at parking violation auctions in New York and in L.A., as mentioned earlier.

However, a great number of assets are sold that will not have any liens on them, and you can find some excellent deals at these auctions.

Depending on your location your efforts to find and attend auctions of this kind will vary. The first thing you should do is to contact the local sheriff and/or marshal and ask them about any and all auctions they may conduct. You will probably find these individuals to be helpful since in many areas the Marshal may receive a percentage of the proceeds. The more he brings in, the more he makes, so he should be interested in helping potential buyers. One of the New York City Marshals has been so busy that his earnings approached $500,000 per year while the Mayor and the Governor only earn $130,000 per year.

Unfortunately, in other locations you will find other marshals or sheriffs to be less than cooperative. In these areas you should get in the habit of scanning the auction and legal notices on a daily basis to catch an advertisement for the upcoming auction. If you attend one of these auctions that happens to be run by a private auctioneer, it is probable that he may handle auctions of this type on a recurrent basis, so ask to be placed on his mailing list for upcoming auctions.

At the risk of sounding repetitive, once you have identified an upcoming auction you must do the following:

1) Make sure you understand the payment terms before you attend the auction. Be prepared to meet all the terms.

2) Inspect the assets. Determine their value. Set a bid price limit based upon your inspection and consider any negative aspects such as liens or time delay for ownership.

3) Register to bid if required.

4) Bid with your wits about you to avoid paying more than you should. Avoid getting caught by techniques of the auctioneer to raise your bid. Reread Part 1, Chapter 1 of this book. This will help you conduct yourself properly at the auction.

5) Do not go over your bid price limit.

6) Pick up your merchandise as soon as possible and never let the pick up time expire.

7) Ask to be placed on the auctioneers mailing list.

These basic points will help you tremendously in an auction environment. If you combine all the information in this book with your good common sense, you will have a good auction experience. Whether you are interested in attending auctions as an income producing venture or if you just need to pick up an extra car for your kid, you now have the skills to find yourself a deal in acquiring the assets of your choice.

Part Six

PRIVATE SECTOR AUCTIONS

PART SIX

INTRODUCTION

The private sector of auctions contains some of the best and most respected sources of auctions, and some of the least respected. You are probably aware that much of the valuable art on the market is sold through various auction houses. Some of the most valuable things on this earth are sold through the auction process as a first choice. The success of these auctions has spilled over to areas other than the art world. The auction as a means of selling is becoming more popular every day. In the future you will see more numerous and diverse assets being sold at auction.

We will discuss the current and emerging private sector of auctions in this chapter. We hope you will take part in the growth in popularity of this sector. We will alert you to the positive aspects and the pitfalls of dealing with the private sector. Some of the private sector auctions are well established and recognized, and others are new and full of opportunity. Still others are to be identified as blatant marketing ploys and should be avoided.

Please remember one of the keys to your success is your good common sense. Sometimes that seems to be a commodity that is in short supply, but our readers have the knowledge we have provided to help you to be successful. When you see an auction being advertised, I want you to look past the advertisement and see the whole picture. Do not be fooled by slick ad campaigns or be pulled in by buzz words. Let me give you an example.

One auction firm I know specializes in real estate sales. When they advertise they state that they "will sell 73 condominiums at auction and 6 will be sold absolute regardless of price." Well, you might think this may be the opportunity of a lifetime. It's not. It is just a way to advertise that includes a phrase like "sold absolute regardless of price" which will motivate people to attend the auction. When they have a large quantity of assets to sell it is not even a gamble for them to assume they can sell at least 10 of those assets at a fair price. So what they do is to put the first condo on the block and sell it. They are bound to get a high price for it due to the large turnout their advertising always generates. When the first condo is sold to the highest bidder they say that condo was sold "absolute". The first six sales are the ones that are declared to be absolute. As I mentioned in PART ONE, CHAPTER 5 of this book, under bidding strategy, the bid prices will decrease for similar assets as the auction proceeds. So you see, this great offer of selling a few assets absolutely is no skin off their nose because the first few sales are normally higher priced. When they get to the rest of the condos they will have a reserve price on them to protect themselves from giving anything away.

If you use the knowledge and tricks of the trade discussed in this book, along with a good helping of your common sense, you will be on top of the auction situation, not bowled over by it. Remember, the auctioneer is a salesman, and the ad writers are advertising executives whose job it is to motivate you to attend and spend at an auction. I believe you should attend, but never spend more than your carefully considered bid price limit.

PART 6

CHAPTER 1

WELL ESTABLISHED AUCTION HOUSES

We have all heard about the Sotheby's and Christie's auction houses in New York. These are the premier auction houses in the world. They handle some of the most expensive items and their audience is from all parts of the world. Their reputation is the basis for all of their business, so you can be assured of the most professional and proper treatment at these organizations. They are not the only auction houses worth mentioning. Every city will have a well established auction house.

Many of these auction houses will specialize in a certain type or class of asset. The larger ones have a wide variety of specialties, and a smaller house may only deal in antiques. If you determine that you are in the market for a Monet painting, then you should contact these auction houses. If you happen to find a Monet in your attic then bring it to one of the top auction houses because they will be best suited to sell it for the highest possible dollar value.

You will find all types of assets at these well established auction houses. Some people have made vast fortunes dealing with the assets that are sold at these institutions. You do not have to be in the big leagues to participate in these private sector auctions. You can find a firm that handles items in your price range, although it is fascinating to attend an auction where someone will bid many millions of dollars for a work of art (it gets you dizzy). All of these firms maintain mailing lists and some will even keep you informed by fax or phone of upcoming events if you are a big player in a particular field of interest. I strongly suggest that you enroll or subscribe to these mailing lists. You must be informed on what may be available for auction so that you won't miss an opportunity to buy something fantastic.

For the majority of this book, I have been writing about buying assets at auctions. The other side of the coin is selling your assets at auctions. You can sell just about anything at an auction house that deals with your type of merchandise. You will be charged a commission or a flat fee for the services of the auction house. My opinion on fee structure is to go with a firm that works on commission because they have an incentive to get you the highest dollar price.

If you think you have an asset or a work of art that may be valuable you must contact the PROPER firm to liquidate it. This is extremely important! There are many cases of someone buying a piece of art for thousands of dollars, then reselling it for millions at Sotheby's. How do you think you would feel if you were watching the evening news and saw a report about a work of art that just sold for $11,000,000, only to realize it was that old painting in your Granny's attic that you had so wisely sold for $1,346.69. I don't think the word depression would be adequate.

The moral to this story is to bring anything that even smells valuable to the best firms possible. I have had Sotheby's take a look at some art work, and I was glad I did. They want you to bring assets to them also because they will collect a large commission for liquidating your treasure. Go to the top because if you don't, someone else will. I don't want you to get the impression that you must have a work of art by one of the masters to have it sold. Antiques, rare instruments, etc., etc., may be valuable. You can locate these firms easily because they advertise widely.

PART 6

CHAPTER 2

PRIVATE SECTOR REAL ESTATE AUCTIONS

The use of auctions to sell real estate in the private sector is becoming increasingly popular in the United States. In other countries, like Australia, nearly 90% of all real estate transactions are done through the auction process. The realization of the numerous benefits of auction sales are leading more and more properties to the auction block. The sources of these properties range from developers to private homeowners. As this trend develops, you will have more and more opportunities to buy at an auction.

As the real estate market hit hard times, very resourceful people turned to the auctioning of real estate as a marketing tool. In many instances "necessity became the mother of invention". As buyers became few and far between and the average time for a sale lengthened, a method to speed up the process was desperately needed. People attempting to sell real estate were paying carrying costs on properties that were falling in price. That is not a good situation to be in, and developers had the problem multiplied by the number of unsold units they had.

The auction process allowed these people to get their properties sold, but they had to make some adjustments to their way of doing business. The first thing they had to do was to abandon the inflated asking prices that are traditional when dealing through a Realtor. No one would come to an auction that required a ridiculously high opening bid for a property. These sellers had to establish a base price that would get them out of the situation they were in. The alternative was to hold out for the old high price and keep piling on the carrying costs. The motivation for the seller to establish a base price that should sell in today's market was financial and emotional because it would free them from a problem property.

Once the realization and the determination was made to sell, the auction process enabled these people to sell their property quickly and at a level that was acceptable to them. Most sellers put a reserve price on the property to protect themselves from giving the property away, but these reserves are normally much lower than the asking prices they had on the properties.

The Terms and Conditions you will encounter in these types of auctions will vary widely. Basically they will be tailored to the seller's needs. You must pay special attention to all the terms and be prepared to meet them. As with all Real Estate transactions, I suggest you retain an attorney to protect your interests in these dealings.

These are some of the easiest auctions to find out about. Since they are being used as a marketing tool and not a mandated form of liquidation, they are advertised heavily. The advertisements normally appear in the real estate sections of your local newspapers along with other means of publicity. The sellers are taking an unusual step to sell their property and your attendance is a main requirement for them to be successful, so they will try to get the word out.

I want you to be aware that many sellers think and hope they will be able to sell their property at a high price because it is going to auction. Although I have been at auctions and witnessed assets sell for more than they are worth, this is the exception rather than the rule. These sellers may waste your time by placing an unreasonably high reserve price on the property, and it will not sell unless someone with no idea of what they are doing buys the asset. I don't want my readers to get upset that you didn't buy the asset because it went for more than your bid price limit. You are far better off by wasting some of your time at the auction than wasting your money as the unwitting buyer.

These types of auctions may offer you some good opportunities, but they should be a low priority for you. They are not forced or ordered sales, as some of the other categories I have discussed. You are dealing with a private entity or individual that is trying, sometimes desperately, to liquidate an asset. These assets may not sell if the expectations of the seller are out of line. These auctions are worth looking into, but it is highly unlikely you will get the type of deal that would be worth mentioning in this book. There are other sufficient sources where your potential for savings is greater.

PART 6

CHAPTER 3

BANKS, FINANCE COMPANIES AND PRIVATE LENDERS

The auctions held by or at the order of banks, finance companies and private lenders are excellent sources for all sorts of assets. These companies fund the purchase of assets, and these assets are pledged as security for the loans. Whenever the borrower fails to repay the loan the lender will try to recoup its investment by selling the assets which were pledged as security for the loan. This is where the auction buyer has the opportunity to buy the assets at normally good prices. The Lender is primarily concerned with recouping the amount of their loan plus costs of liquidation, and are not very concerned with any amount above that which would go to the borrower.

In many cases the Lender only gets a portion of their loan recouped and will take a loss. The value of the underlying assets may be less than the loan value that is outstanding on the property. That has been the case in the early 1990's with real estate. Banks and finance companies have been increasing their REO's (real estate owned by the bank) significantly because they do not want to take the loss on the property. In normal circumstances, at an auction for repossessed or foreclosed assets, the bank will bid in its interest (loan amount) on the property and then the bidding would go up from there. The next bid after the bank's would take the bank out by having the new bidder pay an amount that is sufficient to pay the bank what it is owed.

As a result of the real estate market crash, the normal course of events described above was not happening. When the bank bids in its interest no one would bid any higher, so the bank would then own the property. Their decision to bid in their interest at a level that was so high in the reality of the current market conditions in most cases just delayed the inevitable. Sooner or later the bank would sell off the property and take their loss and stop gambling on the condition of the real estate market. I guess they just would not admit they had made a mistake when they originally evaluated the loan. Some banks have adopted a policy to take their lumps on a loan that has gone bad sooner rather than later. These banks will accept the "Market Value" of the asset being established by the auction and not their unrealistic estimate of the assets value.

You will find all types of assets, from business fixtures to cars, boats and planes, at these auctions. A huge number of cars are repossessed and sold every week in this country. The lien holder, either a bank, finance company or lease company will sell at auction the vehicles they repossess. Some companies will sell these vehicles in an open public auction, and others may sell them through restricted auctions which require you to be a car dealer to attend. Every year, all makes and models will be available in a range of conditions and mileage. If you buy a relatively new car, the warrantee can be transferred to you.

The type of title you will receive will depend on your state's regulation regarding repossessed vehicles. I suggest you speak with the auction company before you attend the auction and confirm their story with your Department of Motor Vehicles about the title transfer. These auctions will normally require payment in cash or certified check at knockdown or they may accept a deposit and give you a few days to pay the balance.

Please follow all my advice in PART ONE of this book when attending the auction and inspecting the vehicles. You can locate auctions of this type in a number of ways.

1) Most of these auctions that are open to the public are advertised in a local paper in the auction or legal section.

2) Contact the banks in your area and ask them what they do with their repossessed assets. They normally have a firm contracted to handle everything for them. If you discover that they use a trade restricted wholesale auction, there are still ways to attend these. The best way is to make yourself a used car dealer. In most states this is a very easy procedure of filling out a few forms and paying a small fee. Then these auctions are open to you. I would only go through this process if I were planning on

using the buying and selling of cars as a business or a serious income boosting hobby.

As for other assets that go to auction as a result of repossession, you will find ample supply of boats and even planes at these auctions. Many assets from the commercial world make their way to these auctions. A loan might have been made to a small business to buy equipment and that equipment might be available if the company ran into trouble. All you need to do is to keep informed on upcoming auctions and you may see something that interests you. Sooner or later, almost anything you could imagine will be sold at an auction.

This segment of the auction world can provide you with more opportunities than you can possibly take advantage of. If you combine this with all the government sector auctions the amount is staggering. I want my readers to pursue these auctions and start saving and making money. I hear stories all the time about a deal this guy made and the money another made at some of these auctions. There is nothing special about these people. They are just like you, but they have the knowledge and the desire to get out there and attend these auctions and find themselves in "the right place at the right time". After reading this book you have a big advantage over someone who didn't, so use your advantage to the fullest.

PART 6

CHAPTER 4

ALL OTHER SOURCES OF AUCTIONS

In the private sector you will encounter all types of auctions. Anyone can hire an auctioneer to attempt to sell anything. You will find great auctions that sell valuable assets at great prices, such as the ones mentioned in the Foreword of this book. You will find bad auctions that try to sell a bunch of junk at high prices. You will find auctions that waste your time. They sounded good, but when you got there they weren't what they seemed. You hopefully won't find terrible auctions that are pure cons run by rip off artists. This variety and the potential for less favorable auctions is a feature of the private sector that is different from the Government sector.

In this sector you will have to be a little skeptical about advertisements that sound too good to be true. There are plenty of auctions from this sector which will be worth your time. It seems that the same auction companies run the same type of auction over and over. After a short time you will be able to realize which auction or auction firm will run a good auction.

The type of assets will vary widely, and you may be surprised by the quality and the quantity that is available. Many corporations will use this sector to sell off surplus assets. This can include office equipment, manufacturing equipment, vehicles, excess or discontinued parts and supplies, etc. In large corporations, when a decision has been made to get out of a particular business, they will usually sell off the division. A small company may not have a significant business to warrant a sale of it as an entity. They will commonly have the equipment that was needed for the business segment they are abandoning that will now become surplus to their firm. This equipment is of no use to them so they will try to sell it off. Many firms are turning to auctions to accomplish this. I have found excellent deals at some of these auctions.

These auctions are usually well advertised by the auction firm that is handling them. Watch for advertisements in your major newspapers for these auctions. These advertisements will normally state the reason for the sale on the top of the ad. You will see things like; "By Order of the Board of Directors" or "Surplus Corporate Assets" and a multitude of other headings describing the type of auction. Once you determine which auction firms handle good sales you should get on their mailing lists and they will keep you informed.

The Terms and Conditions you will encounter at these sales will vary widely. Make sure you understand them completely and be prepared to meet them. With auctions held in the private sector you will have more difficulties in complaining and getting a solution to a problem that may develop. With Government sector auctions, you know that the agency that sponsored the auction will be there for you to complain to. This is not always the case with these private sales. Take every step to insure that you do not have a problem as detailed in other chapters of this book. I have advised you to pick up you merchandise as soon as possible, but I would like you to try to bring your purchase with you right after the sale. This will go a long way in protecting you.

Part Seven

DIRECTORY OF FEDERAL AGENCIES

THE UNITED STATES MARSHALS

The U. S. Marshal does not maintain a mailing list. Some of the offices listed below are starting to provide a voice mail recorded service to handle inquiries regarding auctions. This method of providing auction information may be expanded if the system achieves good results. The majority of offices would prefer you to write to them with inquiries regarding auctions of assets. You should be as brief as possible and enclose a self addressed stamped envelope. Address your letter to the forfeiture specialist of seized assets.

Your letter should request any information on upcoming sales and/or the name of the auction firm that is contracted to handle the sales for them. You may get a response from some of these offices that will instruct you to look for public notices in certain newspapers. Also ask them what newspaper their notices run in and if a particular day of the week is used. When you find out which auction company will handle the sale contact them and get on their mailing list. Since the USMS will use different auction companies, unless they are contracted long term, you will have to keep on top of this. It is a little leg work but it is worth it.

ALABAMA

    U.S. Marshal Northern District

    1729 5th Ave. North

    Room 240

    Birmingham, Alabama 35203

THE WORLD OF AUCTIONS

U.S. Marshal Middle District

P. O. Drawer 4249

Montgomery, Alabama 36103-4249

U.S. Marshal Southern District

P. O, Box 343

Mobile, Alabama 36601

ALASKA

U.S. Marshal

222 West 7thn #28

Anchorage, Alaska 99513

ARKANSAS

U.S. Marshal Eastern District

600 West Capital

Room 449, P. O. Box 8

Little Rock, Arkansas 72203

U.S. Marshal Western District

243 U.S. Post Office

6th Street and Rogers Ave.

Fort Smith, Arkansas 72902

ARIZONA

U.S. Marshal

230 N. 1st. Ave.

Suite 8201

Phoenix, Arizona 85025

COLORADO

    U.S. Marshal

    1929 Stout Street

    Denver, Colorado 80294

CONNECTICUT

    U.S. Marshal

    450 Main Street

    Hartford, Connecticut 06103

    (This district has a few satellite offices)

CALIFORNIA

    U.S. Marshal Central District

    312 North Spring Street

    Los Angeles, California 90012

    Telephone #: 213-894-2484

They have an automated telephone system for you to call for auction information. You must use a touch tone phone.

    U.S. Marshal Southern District

    U.S. Court House

    940 Front Street; Room LLB71

    San Diego, California 92189

    U.S. Marshal Eastern District

    650 Capital Mall; Suite 1020

    Sacramento, California 95814

THE WORLD OF AUCTIONS

    U.S. Marshal Northern District
    450 Golden Gate Ave.
    P. O. Box 36056
    San Francisco, California 94102

DELAWARE
    U.S. Marshal
    4311 U.S. Courthouse
    844 King Street
    Willmington, Delaware 19801

FLORIDA
    U.S. Marshal Southern District
    301 N. Miami Ave., Room 205
    Miami, Florida 33128

    U.S. Marshal Middle District
    P. O. Box 2907
    Tampa, Florida 33601

    U.S. Marshal Northern District
    110 East Park Ave.
    P. O. Box 10229
    Tallahassee, Florida 32302

GEORGIA

    U.S. Marshal Northern District

    75 Spring Street, Room 1669 Atlanta, Georgia 30303

    U.S. Marshal Southern District

    P. O. Box 9765

    Savannah, Georgia 31412

    U.S. Marshal Middle District

    P. O. Box 7

    Macon, Georgia 31202

HAWAII

    U.S. Marshal

    P. O. Box 50184

    Honolulu, Hawaii 96850

IDAHO

    U.S. Marshal

    P. O. Box 010

    550 West Fort Street

    Boise, Idaho 83724

ILLINOIS

    U.S. Marshal Northern District

    219 South Dearborn

    Chicago, Illinois   62444

U.S. Marshal Central District
P. O. Box 156
600 East Monroe Street
Springfield, Illinois 62705

U.S. Marshal Southern District
750 Missouri Ave., Suite 027
East St. Louis, Illinois 62201

INDIANA

U.S. Marshal Southern District
46 East Ohio
Indianapolis, Indiana 46204

U.S. Marshal Northern District
233 Federal Building
204 South Main Street
Southbend, Indiana 46601

IOWA

U.S. Marshal Southern District
208 U.S. Courthouse
East 1st and Walnut
Des Moines, Iowa 50309

U.S. Marshal Northern District
101 1st. Street S. E.
320 Federal Building
Cedar Rapids, Iowa 52401

KANSAS

    U.S. Marshal

    444 S. E. Quincy

    Topeka, Kansas 66683

KENTUCKY

    U.S. Marshal Western District

    601 West Broad

    114 U.S. Courthouse

    Louisville, Kentucky 40202

    U.S. Marshal Eastern District

    P. O. Box 30

    Lexington, Kentucky 40501 Louisiana

    U.S. Marshal Western District

    P. O. Box 53

    Shreveport, Louisiana 71161

    U.S. Marshal Eastern District

    C-600 U.S. Courthouse

    500 Camp Street

    New Orleans, Louisiana 70130

    U.S. Marshal Middle District

    P. O. Box 3653

    Baton Rouge, Louisiana 70821

MAINE
>U.S. Marshal
>156 Federal Street
>Room 223
>Portland, Maine 04101

MARYLAND
>U.S. Marshal
>101 West Lumbard Street
>Baltimore, Maryland 21201

MASSACHUSETTS
>U.S. Marshal
>1516 U.S. Courthouse
>Congress & Water Street
>Boston Massachusetts 02109

MICHIGAN
>U.S. Marshal Eastern District
>231 West Lafayette Street
>Federal Building Room 120 Detroit, Michigan 48226

>U.S. Marshal Western District
>544 Federal Building
>110 Michigan Ave.
>Grand Rapids, Michigan 49503

MINNESOTA

    U.S. Marshal
    523 U.S. Courthouse
    110 South 4th Street
    Minneapolis, Minnesota 55401

MISSISSIPPI

    U.S. Marshal Southern District
    P. O. Box 959
    Jackson, Mississippi 39205

    U.S. Marshal Northern District
    P. O. Box 887
    Oxford, Mississippi 38655

MISSOURI

    U.S. Marshal Western District
    509 U.S. Courthouse
    811 Grand Ave
    Kansas City, Missouri 64106

    U.S. Marshal Eastern District
    108 U.S. Courthouse
    1114 Market Street
    St. Louis, Missouri 63101

MONTANA
    U.S. Marshal
    5110 Federal Building
    316 North 26th Street
    Billings Montana 59101

NEBRASKA
    U.S. Marshal
    215 North 17th Street
    Room 8121
    Omaha, Nebraska 68102

NEVADA
    U.S. Marshal
    300 Las Vegas Blvd. South
    Room 42-40
    Las Vegas, Nevada 89101

NEW HAMPSHIRE
    U.S. Marshal
    55 Pleasant St.
    P. O. Box 1435
    Concord, New Hampshire 03301-1435

NEW JERSEY
    U.S. Marshal
    P. O. Box 186
    Newark, New Jersey 07101

NEW MEXICO
   U.S. Marshal
   P. O. Box 157
   Albuquerque, New Mexico 87103

NEW YORK
   U. S. Marshal Southern District
   1 St. Andrews Plaza
   New York, New York 10007

   U.S. Marshal Eastern District
   225 Cadman Plaza
   Brooklyn, New York

   U.S. Marshal Western District
   129 U.S. Courthouse
   68 Court Street
   Buffalo, New York 14202

   U.S. Marshal Northern District
   213 Federal Building
   10 Broad Street
   Utica, New York 13501

NORTH CAROLINA
   U.S. Marshal Western District
   P.O. Box 710
   Asheville, North Carolina 28802

U.S. Marshal Eastern District
P.O. Box 25648
Raleigh, North Carolina 27611

U.S. Marshal Middle District
P.O. Box 1528
Greensboro, North Carolina 27402

NORTH DAKOTA

U.S. Marshal
P.O. Box 2424
Fargo, North Dakota 58108

OHIO

U.S. Marshal Northern District
201 Superior Ave.
B-1 U.S. Courthouse
Cleveland, OHIO 44114

U.S. Marshal Southern District
425 U.S. Courthouse
85 Marconi Blvd.
Columbus, Ohio 43215

OKLAHOMA

U.S. Marshal Eastern District
P.O. Box 732
Muskogee, Oklahoma 74402

U.S. Marshal Western District
P.O. Box 886
Oklahoma City, Oklahoma 73101

U.S. Marshal Northern District
P.O. Box 1097
Tulsa, Oklahoma 74101

OREGON
U.S. Marshal
620 Southwest Main Street
Portland, Oregon 97205

PENNSYLVANIA
U.S. Marshal Eastern District
601 Market Street
Room 2110
Philadelphia, Pennsylvania 19106

U.S. Marshal Western District
539 U.S. Courthouse
Pittsburgh, Pennsylvania 15219

U.S. Marshal Middle District
231 Federal Building
Washington and Lylden Streets
Scranton, Pennsylvania 18501

THE WORLD OF AUCTIONS

PUERTO RICO
> U.S. Marshal
> P.O. Box 887; Adorey Station
> Adorey, Puerto Rico 00919-887

RHODE ISLAND
> U.S. Marshal
> c/o U.S. Courthouse
> 1 Kennedy Plaza
> Providence, Rhode Island 02903

SOUTH CAROLINA
> U.S. Marshal
> P.O. Box 1174
> Columbia, South Carolina 29202

SOUTH DAKOTA
> U.S. Marshal
> 400 South Phillips Street
> Room 216
> Sioux Falls, South Dakota 57102

TENNESSEE
> U.S. Marshal Eastern District
> P.O. Box 551
> Knoxville, Tennessee 37901

U.S. Marshal Western District
160 North Main Street
Memphis, Tennessee 38103

U.S. Marshal Middle District
801 Broadway
Nashville, Tennessee 37203

TEXAS

U.S. Marshal Northern District
1100 Commerce Street
Dallas, Texas 75242

U.S. Marshal Southern District
101 30 U.S. Courthouse
515 Rusk Ave.
Houston, Texas 77002

U.S. Marshal Western District
235 U.S. Courthouse
655 East Durango Blvd.
San Antonio, Texas 78206

UNITED STATES VIRGIN ISLANDS

U.S. Marshal
P.O. Box 9018
St. Thomas, Virgin Islands 00801

UTAH

U.S. Marshal
P.O. Box 1234
Salt Lake City, Utah 84110

VIRGINIA

U.S. Marshal Eastern District
P.O. Box 20227
Alexandria, Virginia 22302

U.S. Marshal Western District
P.O. Box 2280
Roanoke, Virginia 24004

WASHINGTON

U.S. Marshal Western District
1010 5th Ave., Room 300
Seattle, Washington 98104

U.S. Marshal Eastern District
888 U.S. Courthouse
W 920 Riverside Ave.
Spokane, Washington 99201

WASHINGTON D.C.

U.S. Marshal
600 Army Navy Drive
Arlington, Virginia 22202
Attn.: Seized Assets

WEST VIRGINIA

    U.S. Marshal Southern District
    P.O. Box 2667
    Charleston, West Virginia 25330

    U.S. Marshal Northern District
    P.O. Box 1454
    Elkins, West Virginia 26241

    U.S. Marshal
    P.O. Box 726
    Wheelings, West Virginia 26003

WISCONSIN

    U.S. Marshal Western District
    120 North Henry Street, Room 440
    Madison, Wisconsin 53703

    U.S. Marshal Eastern District
    517 East Wisconsin Ave, Suite 38
    Milwaukee, Wisconsin 53202

WYOMING

    U.S. Marshal
    2120 Capital Ave., Room 2124
    Cheyenne, Wyoming 82003

THE UNITED STATES CUSTOMS SERVICE

Customs is one of the best sources for assets of all types. They have the largest inventory of boats and planes of any federal agency and have thousands of vehicles that are sold off at auctions. In addition to these popular items, Customs has everything imaginable for sale that didn't clear import for one reason or another. Customs auctions should be one of your high priority auctions for you to attend on a regular basis.

Customs currently uses a private contractor to handle the custody and disposition of all their assets on a national basis. The current contractor is EG&G DYNATREND. Customs will review all of its contracts on a regular basis and may choose another firm to handle their assets. If that happens EG&G DYNATREND should refer your inquiry to the new contractor or you can contact U. S. Customs directly as listed below.

To contact EG&G DYNATREND:

EG&G DYNATREND

Central Headquarters

2300 Clarendon Blvd., Suite 705

Arlington, VA 22201

Tel (703) 351-7880

Fax (703) 351-9899

MAILING LIST: They maintain a mailing list that you can and should subscribe to. You can either get the East or West regions of the country for $25 per year or you can get the whole country for $50. This list will give you sales flyers for all sales.

THE RESOLUTION TRUST CORPORATION

If you want a house, commercial property or land then you must contact RTC on a regular basis to see what they have. They are not limited to real estate, all of the furniture, fixtures and equipment of all of the banks they took over will be sold as well. They have billions of dollars of assets that will be sold either by direct negotiated sale or by auction. The majority of the assets are being sold at auction. RTC will offer you financing on certain properties and offer you other incentives such as money off for cash sales. Look into all their programs and take advantage of them.

The RTC is a rapidly changing organization. Their incentive programs are always in a state of change so you will have to keep on top of them. Their offices change frequently also. I will list the offices that exist today for your convenience. I suggest that you ask them if the office you are speaking with is responsible for the liquidation of all the assets in your geographic area. You should also keep after them about auction and asset information. Do not rely on being placed on a mailing list with RTC, you may find that your subscription gets lost in the shuffle.

Since you and I are paying for the bailout that the RTC is handling, you might as well get something out of it by buying some of the assets at great prices. Remember you must keep after the RTC so as not to miss anything.

RTC SALES CENTER DIRECTORY

    National Sales Center

    801 17th Street, NW

    Suite 200

    Washington, DC 20434

    (202) 416-4200

EASTERN REGION

    Atlanta Sales Center

    245 Peach Tree Center, N.E.

    Atlanta, Georgia 30303

    Telephone #; 404-225-5088

    800-782-7355

Covers: Alabama, District of Columbia, Georgia, Maryland, North Carolina, South Carolina, Tennessee, Virginia and West Virginia.

    Valley Forge Sales Center

    1000 Adams Street

    Norristown, Pennsylvania 19403

    Telephone #: 215-631-4819

    800-782-6326

Covers: Connecticut, Delaware, Maine, Massachusetts, New Hampshire, Pennsylvania, Rhode Island and Vermont.

    Metropolitan New York/New Jersey Sales Center

    300 Davidson Avenue

    Somerset, New Jersey 08873

    Telephone #: 908-805-4000

    800-248-9472

Covers: New York and New Jersey.

    Tampa Sales Center

    4300 West Cypress Street

    Suite 175

    Tampa, Florida 33607

    Telephone #: 813-870-7200

    800-777-8777

Covers: Florida, Puerto Rico and Virgin Islands

THE WORLD OF AUCTIONS

NORTH CENTRAL REGION

    Kansas City Sales Center

    4900 Main Street, 1st Floor

    Kansas City, Missouri 64112

    Telephone #: 816-968-7355

    800-822-7355

Covers: Iowa, Kansas and Missouri

    Baton Rouge Sales Center

    100 St. James Street

    Depot Building

    Baton Rouge, Louisiana 70821

    504-339-1375

    800-477-8790

Covers: Louisiana and Mississippi.

    Chicago Sales Center

    25 N.W. Point Blvd

    Elk Grove Village, Illinois 60007

    708-290-7555; 800-388-7822

Covers: Illinois, Indiana, Kentucky, Michigan and Ohio.

    Minneapolis Sales Center

    3400 Yankee Drive

    Eagan, Minnesota 55122

    Telephone #: 612-683-4600

    800-876-7253

Covers: Alaska, Idaho, Minnesota, Montana, Nebraska, North Dakota, Oregon, South Dakota, Washington, Wisconsin and Wyoming.

>Tulsa Sales Center
>321 South Boston
>P.O. Box 2269
>Tulsa, Oklahoma 74103
>Telephone #: 918-587-7600
>800-759-3342

Covers: Oklahoma and Arkansas.

SOUTH WESTERN DISTRICT

>Dallas Sales Center
>3500 Maple Avenue
>Reverchon Plaza, 18th Floor
>Dallas, Texas 75219
>Telephone #: 214-443-4673
>800-782-4674

Covers: Northeast Texas.

>Austin Sales Center
>4303 Victory Drive
>Suite 205
>Austin, Texas 78704
>Telephone #: 512-443-9464
>800-677-3044

Covers: Central Texas.

THE WORLD OF AUCTIONS

Houston Sales Center
2223 West Loop South
Houston, Texas 77027
713-888-2900; 800-879-8492

Covers: Southeast Texas.

San Antonio Sales Center
10100 Reunion Place, 1st Floor
San Antonio, Texas 78216
512-525-6500; 800-283-9158

Covers: Western Texas.

WESTERN REGION

Denver Sales Center
1515 Arapahoe Street
Tower 3, Suite 800
Denver, Colorado 80202
303-556-6678; 800-542-6135; 800-437-1842

Covers: Colorado, New Mexico and Utah.

Irvine Sales Center
4000 MacArthur Blvd.
Newport Beach, California 92660
714-852-7600; 800-926-6390

Covers: California, Hawaii and Guam

Phoenix Sales Center

2910 North 44th Street

Phoenix, Arizona 85018

602-381-3400; 800-866-1220

Covers: Arizona and Nevada

Tucson Sales Center

160 North Stone Avenue

2nd Floor

Tuscon, Arizona 85701

602-622-8259; 800-223-1863

Covers: Southern Arizona

THE GENERAL SERVICES ADMINISTRATION (GSA)

The General Services Administration handles the sale of surplus assets for most of the Federal government. They utilize in-house auctioneers and they offer in-house mailing lists that you can be placed on. To be included in GSA mailings either call or write to the region listed below that handles your area. They also have telephone "Hot-Lines" to detail upcoming auctions. Get in the habit of calling these numbers on a regular basis.

Many people think GSA will only handle used typewriters and associated boring assets. This is not the case. I have seen everything from exotic cars to yachts being sold at GSA auctions. The way the regulations are written all the "flash" cars, (cars used by federal agents for undercover work) are turned over to GSA for sale. Some of these cars are excellent and even exotic models that offer you a good opportunity to purchase.

WASHINGTON D.C. REGION

    GSA

    6808 Loisdale Road

    Building A

    Springfield, VA 22150

    703-557-0384

    Hot-line #: 703-557-7796

REGION ONE

    GSA

    10 Causeway Street #2FBP-1

    Boston, MA 02222

    617-565-8100

    Hot-line #: 617-565-7326

Covers: Connecticut, Maine, Massachusetts, New Hampshire, Rhode Island and Vermont.

REGION TWO

    GSA

    26 Federal Plaza

    #2FB-2, Room 20-100D

    New York, NY 10278

    212-264-3590

    Hot-line #: 212-264-4823

Covers: New Jersey, Puerto Rico, Virgin Islands and New York.

REGION THREE

    GSA

    Surplus Sales Division

    9th & Market Streets

    P. O. Box 1289

    Room 5156

    Philadelphia, PA 19106

    215-597-5674

    Hot-line #: 215-597-7253

Covers: Delaware, Pennsylvania, Virginia, West Virginia and Maryland.

THE WORLD OF AUCTIONS

REGION FOUR

> GSA
>
> Sales Division
>
> 401 West Peach Tree Street, N.W.
>
> Atlanta, GA 30365
>
> 404-331-3064
>
> Hot-line #: 404-331-5177

Covers: Alabama, Florida, Georgia, Kentucky, Mississippi, North Carolina, South Carolina and Tennessee.

REGION FIVE

> GSA; Federal Suppy Service Bureau
>
> Sales Services, Mail Staff 34-5
>
> 230 South Dearborn Street
>
> Chicago, IL 60604
>
> 312-353-5375
>
> Hot-line #: 312-353-0246

Covers: Illinois, Indiana, Michigan, Minnesota, Ohio and Wisconsin.

REGION SIX

> GSA
>
> 4400 College Blvd.
>
> Overland Park, KS 66211
>
> 913-236-2525
>
> Hot-line #: 913-236-2565

Covers: Iowa, Kansas, Missouri and Nebraska

REGION SEVEN

    GSA

    819 Taylor Street

    Room 6E04

    Fort Worth, TX 76102

    817-334-2352

    Hotline #: None available.

Covers: Arkansas, Louisiana, New Mexico, Oklahoma and Texas

REGION EIGHT

    GSA

    Federal Supply Service Bureau

    Personal Property Service

    P. O. Box 25506

    #7FBP-8

    Denver, Colorado 80225

    303-236-7702

    Hot-line #: 303-236-7705

Covers: Colorado, Montana, North Dakota, South Dakota, Utah and Wyoming.

REGION NINE

    GSA

    525 Market Street

    33rd Floor

    San Fransico, CA 94105

    415-744-5245

    Hot-line #: 800-676-7253

Covers: Arizona, California, Guam, Hawaii and Nevada.

THE WORLD OF AUCTIONS

REGION TEN
    GSA
    400 15th Street S.W.
    Auburn, WA 98001
    206-931-7566
    Hotline #: None available.
Covers: Idaho, Oregon and Washington.

THE DEPARTMENT OF DEFENSE

The Department of Defense (DOD) sells assets that it has determined to be surplus to their needs. They utilize two channels for the liquidation of the assets. The first is through one of 140 + local offices called Defense Reutilization Marketing Offices (DRMO's) These offices handle small quantities of assets that are normally sold at sealed bid auctions.

You can contact these offices by calling or writing to the operations headquarters for the district. The DOD currently divides the 140 offices into two regions. These are known as OPERATIONS EAST and OPERATIONS WEST. These central commands have control over all the DRMO's and will provide you with a list of all the DRMO's and a schedule of all the auctions. You must call the DRMO in your location to get detailed information about the assets that are scheduled to be sold. These offices will put you on a mailing list for your convenience.

To contact them, write or call the following addresses:

>DRMS
>
>Operations East
>
>926 Taylor Station Road
>
>P.O. Box 5100
>
>Blacklick, Ohio 43004-5100
>
>614-692-2285

>DRMS
>
>Operations West
>
>500 West 12th Street
>
>Ogden Utah 84407-5001
>
>801-399-7833

The second channel of liquidation is through the National Sales Center. This central office is responsible for large scale sales of assets of all descriptions. You can subscribe to a mailing list, at no cost, to receive asset information and bidding instructions.

The procedure for buying these assets is as follows. You will receive a notification of assets for sale. The location of these assets can be anywhere in the country and you will have a two week period in which to inspect the assets. If you wish to send in a bid you must follow the instructions on your bidding package, which will clearly detail the requirements for bidding. Please pay special attention to the date of submission of your bids. If your bid arrives late you are out of luck! You will also be required to send in a 20% deposit along with your bid, normally in the form of a certified check. If you win the bid then your check will be cashed and applied towards the purchase. If you do not win the bid, your check will be returned to you.

Recently the DOD has allowed credit cards to be used in the bidding and purchase of the assets they liquidate. If you wish to use a credit card for bidding purposes you will be required to complete a form to participate. The use of a credit card is the most convenient method of meeting the deposit requirements of bidding. If your bid wins, then your card is charged. If your bid does not win then nothing will happen to your card. I strongly suggest you use this method of submitting your deposit with your bids, it will save you allot of inconvenience and time.

Whenever you buy an asset from the DOD you will have a specific amount of time to pay for the asset and remove it. Make sure you meet these requirements which can change from sale to sale. If you do not pay your balance due you will forfeit your deposit.

To contact the National Sales Center call or write:

Defense Logistics Agency

DRMS-NSO

2163 Airways Blvd.

Memphis, TN 38114-5211

901-775-6911

THE INTERNAL REVENUE SERVICE (IRS)

The IRS is a relatively good source for auctions. When they sell an asset, they will normally transfer the "rights, title and interest" in the ownership of the asset that has been seized for sale from the delinquent taxpayer. This means that the asset may have one or more liens on it. Look into this carefully and get a clear understanding of the ownership status.

It is easy to contact the IRS for information on their auction sales. The IRS has one national telephone number that you can dial and you will be connected to the IRS telephone center for the state your are calling from. Once you get through ask for any and all auction schedules they may have. You should also request to be placed on any mailing lists they may have.

The IRS is required to advertise all sales in at least one local paper. They are not required to use the same paper over and over again, but for simplicity they normally due.

Ask them which publication they normally use and scan it regularly.

To contact the Internal Revenue Service call: 1-800-829-1040.

THE UNITED STATES POSTAL SERVICE

The United States Postal service will sell assets from two sources. The first source is from the mail that is undeliverable or unclaimed. The second source is their surplus vehicles.

If you are interested in the items that didn't get delivered or picked up then you must contact one of five auction centers where auctions are held on a periodic basis. The auction centers are:

U. S. Postal Service

Auction Center

730 Great Southwest Parkway

Atlanta, GA 30336

404-344-1625

Auctions are held every 6-8 weeks.

U. S. Postal Service

Auction Center

443 East Philmore

St. Paul, MN 55107

612-293-3085

Auctions are held four times per year.

U. S. Postal Service

Auction Center, James A. Farley Building

380 W. 33rd. Street

New York, NY 10019

212-330-2931 Auctions held every two months.

U. S. Postal Service

Auction Center

2970 Market Street

Philadelphia, PA 19014-9652

Auctions are held every three months.

U. S. Postal Service

Auction Center

1300 Evans Avenue

San Francisco, CA

Telephone #: 415-550-6500

Auctions are held every two months.

If you are interested in the auctions of vehicles that are surplus to the needs of the Postal Service, then you must contact the vehicle maintenance center in your state that will sell the vehicles. You can find this office by simply calling your local post office or asking your mail carrier. These auctions are held on a regular basis and have some interesting vehicles in them.

THE FEDERAL DEPOSIT INSURANCE CORPORATION

The FDIC has been increasing the number of auctions they conduct. These auctions are excellent opportunities to purchase everything from office equipment to real property. To contact the FDIC call or write to one of their four regional officies and ask for auction information.

Manager of Liquidations

Federal Deposit Insurance Corporation

30 South Wacker Drive, Suite 3200

Chicago, IL 60606

312-207-0200

Manager of Liquidations

Federal Deposit Insurance Corporation

1910 Pacific Avenue, Suite 1700

Dallas, TX 75202

214-754-0098

Manager of Liquidations

Federal Deposit Insurance Corporation
452 Fifth Avenue
New York, NY 10018
212-704-1200

Manager of Liquidations
Federal Deposit Insurance Corporation
25 Ecker Street, Suite 2300
San Francisco, CA 94105
415-546-1810

Part Eight

THE FEDERAL BANKRUPTCY COURT SYSTEM

The Federal Bankruptcy Court

The bankruptcy court does not handle the auctioning of assets directly. They assign a United States Trustee to handle the sale. You can contact the Trustee's office in your area as listed below. You should ask them if they have a method of keeping you informed about all auctions conducted by the Trustees in their region. (Each region may have as many as 70 Trustees. They are private lawyers who receive a fee for handling the liquidation of bankruptcy assets.) If the regional office does not have a method to keep you informed then you should request a list of all of the Trustees in the region so that you may contact them.

Here is where you may encounter some resistance from the local office. They will normally ask you to write in for a list of their Trustees or require you to come to the office to copy the list. Sometimes you may encounter an employee that will say they do not give out the Trustees name and address because they are "private lawyers". This is WRONG! The Trustees are "public information". Since they are compensated for the services they provide in the handling of a federal bankruptcy case and the fact that the assets from the case must be sold to the "GENERAL PUBLIC", it is your right to know who the Trustees are. Do not give up in your efforts to obtain a list of the Trustees, then you should contact them on a regular basis.

THE WORLD OF AUCTIONS

ADDRESSES OF UNITED STATES TRUSTEE FIELD OFFICES

REGION 1: includes the judicial districts established for the States of Maine, Massachusetts, New Hampshire and Rhode Island.

    E. Frankiln Childress
    United States Trustee

REGIONAL OFFICE

    10 Causeway Street

    Room 472

    Boston, Massachusetts 02222-1043

    617-565-6360

FIELD OFFICES

    66 Pearl Street

    Room 322

    Portland,

    Maine 04101

    44 Front Street

    Suite 440

    Worcester, Massachusetts 01608

66 Hanover Street
Suite 302
Manchester, New Hampshire 03101

REGION 2: includes the judicial districts established for the States of Connecticut, New York and Vermont.

Arthur J. Gonzalez
Acting United States Trustee
REGIONAL OFFICE
80 Broad Street
3rd Floor
New York, New York 10004
Telephone #: 212-668-2200

FIELD OFFICES

42 Delaware Avenue
Suite 100
Buffalo, New York 14202

825 East Gate Avenue
Suite 304
Garden City, New York 11530

50 Chapel Street
First Floor
Albany, New York 12207

THE WORLD OF AUCTIONS

105 Court Street

Room 402

New Haven, Connecticut 06511

100 State Street

Room 609

Rochester, New York 14614

10 Broad Street

Room 105

Utica, New York 13501

REGION 3: Includes the judicial districts established for the States of Delaware, New Jersey and Pennsylvania.

Thomas E. Ross

United States Trustee

REGIONAL OFFICE

601 Walnut Street

Room 950 W

Philadelphia, Pennsylvania 19106

Telephone #: 215-597-4411

FIELD OFFICES

225 Market Street

Suite 503

Harrisburg, Pennsylvania 17101

60 Park Place

Suite 210

Newark, New Jersey 07102

1000 Liberty Avenue

Room 319

Pittsburgh, Pennsylvania 15222

REGION 4: includes the judicial districts established for the States of Maryland, South Carolina, Virginia, West Virginia and the District of Columbia.

David R. Duncan

Acting United States Trustee

REGIONAL OFFICE

1201 Main Street

Room 2440

Columbia, South Carolina 29201

803-765-5599

FIELD OFFICES

115 S. Union Street

Room 210

Alexandria, Virginia 22314

200 Granby Street

Room 625

Norfolk, Virginia 23510

THE WORLD OF AUCTIONS

210 Franklin Road, SW
Room 806
Roanoke, Virginia 24011

500 Virginia Street, East
Room 590
Charleston, West Virginia 25301

51 Monroe Street
Plaza Two
Rockville, Maryland 20850

31 Hopkins Plaza
Room G-13
Baltimore, Maryland 21201

1204 E. Main Street
4th Floor
Richmond, Virginia 23217-2246

115 S. Union Street
Room 210
Alexandria. Virginia 22314

REGION 5: includes the judicial districts established for the States of Louisiana and Mississippi.

    Victoria E. Young

    United States Trustee

REGIONAL OFFICE

400 Poydras Street

Suite 1820

New Orleans, Louisiana 70130

504-589-4018

FIELD OFFICES

500 Fannin Street

Room 3B12

Shreveport, Louisiana 71101-3099

100 W. Capital Street

Suite 1232

Jackson, Mississippi 39269

REGION 6: includes the judicial districts established for the Northern District of Texas and the Eastern District of Texas.

William T. Neary

United States Trustee

REGIONAL OFFICE

1100 Commerce Street

Room 9C60

Dallas, Texas 75242

214-767-8967

THE WORLD OF AUCTIONS

FIELD OFFICE

    110 N. College Avenue

    Room 300

    Tyler, Texas 75702

REGION 7: includes the judicial districts established for the Southern District of Texas and the Western District of Texas.

    Christine A. March

    Acting United States Trustee

REGIONAL OFFICE

    440 Louisiana Street

    Suite 2500

    Houston Texas 77002

    713-238-9650

FIELD OFFICES

    300 E. 8th Street

    Room 906

    Austin, Texas 78701

    615 E, Houston Street

    Room 100

    San Antonio, Texas 78205

REGION 8: includes the judicial districts established for the States of Kentucky and Tennessee.

    E. Franklin Childress

    United States Trustee

REGIONAL OFFICE

    200 Jefferson Avenue

    Suite 400

    Memphis, Tennessee 38103

    Telephone #: 901-544-3251

FIELD OFFICES

    100 East Vine Street

    Suite 803

    Lexington, Kentucky 40507

    601 West Broadway

    Suite 512

    Louisville, Kentucky 40202

    31 East 11th Street

    4th Floor

    Chattanooga, Tennessee 37402

    701 Broadway

    Room 313

    Nashville, Tennessee 37203

REGION 9: includes the judicial districts established for the States of Michigan and Ohio.

    M. Scott Michel

    United States Trustee

REGIONAL OFFICE
> 113 St. Clair Avenue, NE
>
> Suite 200
>
> Clevland, Ohio 44114
>
> 216-522-7800

FIELD OFFICES
> 50 West Broad Street
>
> Suite 325
>
> Columbus, Ohio 43215
>
> 190 Monroe Avenue, NW
>
> Room 200
>
> Grand Rapids, Michigan 49503
>
> 477 Michigan Avenue
>
> Room 1760
>
> Detroit, Michigan 48226
>
> 5th, Main & Walnut Streets
>
> Room 245
>
> Cincinnati, Ohio 45202

REGION 10: includes the Central and Southern Districts of Illinois and the judicial districts established for the State of Indiana.
> Kenneth C. Meeker
>
> United States Trustee

REGIONAL OFFICE
>
    101 W. Ohio Street

    Suite 1000

    Indianapolis, Indiana 46204

    317-226-6101

FIELD OFFICES

    100 East Wayne Street

    Room 555

    South Bend, Indiana 46601

    100 NE Monroe Street

    Room 333

    Peoria, Illinois 61602

REGION 11: includes the Northern District of Illinois and the judicial districts established for the State of Wisconsin.

    M. Scott Michel

    United States Trustee

REGIONAL OFFICE

    175 West Jackson Boulevard

    Room A-1335

    Chicago, Illinois 60604

    312-886-5785

THE WORLD OF AUCTIONS

FIELD OFFICES

    14 West Mifflin Street

    Room 310

    Madison, Wisconsin 53703

    517 East Wisconsin Avenue

    Room 430

    Milwaukee, Wisconsin 53202

REGION 12: includes the judicial districts established for the States of Minnesota, Iowa, North Dakota and South Dakota.

    Wesley B. Huisinga

    United States Trustee

REGIONAL OFFICE

    425 Second Street, SE

    Room 675

    Cedar Rapids, Iowa 52401

    Telephone #: 319-364-2211

FIELD OFFICES

    210 Walnut Street

    Room 517

    Des Moines, Iowa 50309

    331 Second Avenue

    Suite 540

    Minneapolis, Minnesota 55401

230 S. Philips Avenue

Suite 502

Sioux Falls, South Dakota 57102

REGION 13: includes the judicial districts established for the States of Arkansas, Nebraska and Missouri.

John R. Stonitsch

United States Trustee

REGIONAL OFFICE

911 Walnut Street

Room 806

Kansas City, Missouri 64106 Telephone #: 816-426-7959

FIELD OFFICES

815 Olive Street

Room 324

St. Louis, Missouri 63101

210 S. 16th Street

Suite 450

Omaha, Nebraska 68102

500 S. Broadway

Suite 201

Little Rock, Arkansas 72201

REGION 14: includes the District of Arizona

Adrianne Kalyna

United States Trustee

320 N. Central Avenue

Room 100

Phoenix, Arizona 85004

REGION 15: includes the Southern District of California and the judicial districts established for the State of Hawaii, and for Guam and the Commonwealth of the Northern Mariana Islands.

Sandra J. Wittman

United States Trustee

REGIONAL OFFICE

101 West Broadway

Suite 440

San Diego, California 92101

619-557-5013

FIELD OFFICES

300 Ala Moana Boulevard

Room 6321B

Honolulu, Hawaii 96850

238 Archbishop Flores

Room 805

Agana, Guam 96910

REGION 16: includes the Central District of California.

Marcy J. K. Tiffany

United States Trustee

REGIONAL OFFICE

    221 N. Figueroa

    Room 800

    Los Angeles, California 90012

    213-894-6811

FIELD OFFICES

    600 W. Santa Ana Boulevard

    Room 501

    Santa Ana, California 92701

    699 N. Arrowhead Avenue

    Room 106

    San Bernardino, California 92401

REGION 17: includes the Eastern and Northern Districts of California and the judicial district established for the State of Nevada.

    Mark St. Angelo

    Acting United States Trustee

REGIONAL OFFICE

    601 Van Ness Avenue

    Suite 2008

    San Francisco, California 94102

    415-556-7900

FIELD OFFICES

> 600 Las Vegas Boulevard, S.
> Suite 430
> Las Vegas, Nevada 89101

> 350 South Center Street
> Suite 280
> Reno, Nevada 89501

> 280 South First Street
> Room 268
> San Jose, California 95113

> 915 "L" Street
> Suite 1150
> Sacramento, California 95814

> 1130 "O" Street
> Suite 1110
> Fresno, California 93721

> 1401 Lakeside Drive
> Suite 1260
> Oakland, California 94612

REGION 18: includes the judicial districts established for the States of Alaska, Idaho, Montana, Oregon and Washington.

> Mary Jo Heston
> United States Trustee

REGIONAL OFFICE
> 1200 6th Avenue
> Room 600
> Seattle, Washington 98101
> 206-553-2000

FIELD OFFICES
> 851 SW 6th Avenue
> Suite 1300
> Portland, Oregon 97204
>
> North 221 Wall Street
> Suite 538
> Spokane, Washington 99201
>
> 301 Central Avenue
> Suite 204
> Great Falls, Montana 59401
>
> 605 W. Fourth Avenue
> Suite 258
> Anchorage, Alaska 99501
>
> 44 West Broadway
> Suite 500
> Eugene, Oregon 97401

304 N. Eighth Street

Room 347

Boise, Idaho 83702

REGION 19: includes the judicial districts established for the States of Colorado, Utah and Wyoming.

David D. Bird

United States Trustee

REGIONAL OFFICE

721 19th Street

Suite 408

Denver, Colorado 80202

303-844-5188

FIELD OFFICES

9 Exchange Place

Suite 100

Salt Lake City, Utah 84111

2120 Capital Avenue

Room 7008

Cheyenne, Wyoming 82001

REGION 20: includes the judicial districts established for the States of Kansas, New Mexico and Oklahoma.

John E. Foulston

United States Trustee

REGIONAL OFFICE
>   401 North Market Street
>
>   Room 180
>
>   Wichita, Kansas 67202
>
>   316-269-6637

FIELD OFFICES
>   201 NW Dean A. McGee Avenue
>
>   Room 516
>
>   Oklahoma City, Oklahoma 73102
>
>   111 West Fifth Street
>
>   Room 900
>
>   Tulsa, Oklahoma 74103
>
>   320 Central Avenue, SW
>
>   Room 34
>
>   Albuquerque, New Mexico 87103

REGION 21: includes the judicial districts established for the States of Florida, Georgia and for the Commonwealth of Puerto Rico and the Virgin Islands of the United States.

>   Donald F. Walton
>
>   Acting United States Trustee

REGIONAL OFFICE
>   75 Spring Street, SW
>
>   Suite 362
>
>   Atlanta, Georgia 30303
>
>   404-331-4437

FIELD OFFICES

51 SW First Avenue
Room 1204
Miami, Florida 33130

222 W. Oglethorpe Avenue
Suite 302
Savannah, Georgia 31401

4921 Memorial Highway
Room 340
Tampa, Florida 33634

Chardon Street
Room 638
Hato Rey, Puerto Rico 00918

433 Cherry Street
Suite 510
Macon, Georgia 31201

227 N. Bronough Street
Room 1047
Tallahassee, Florida 32301

135 West Central Boulevard
Suite 620
Orlando, Florida 32801

The States of North Carolina and Alabama are excluded from the United States Trustee Program until October 1, 2002.